Xenophon's Socratic Discourse

Other Titles of Interest from St. Augustine's Press

Gerhart Niemeyer, *Between Nothingness and Paradise*

Plato, *The Symposium of Plato: The Shelley Translation* (translated by Percy Bysshe Shelley)

Aristotle, *Aristotle – On Poetics* (translated by Seth Benardete and Michael Davis)

Michael Davis, *The Poetry of Philosophy: On Aristotle's* Poetics

Rémi Brague, *Eccentric Culture: A Theory of Western Civilization*

Roger Scruton, *An Intelligent Person's Guide to Modern Culture*

Roger Scruton, *On Hunting*

Roger Scruton, *The Meaning of Conservatism*

Josef Pieper, *Leisure, the Basis of Culture*

Josef Pieper, *Enthusiasm and Divine Madness: On the Platonic Dialogue* Phaedrus

Stanley Rosen, *Nihilism: A Philosophical Essay*

Stanley Rosen, *The Ancients and the Moderns: Rethinking Modernity*

Stanley Rosen, *Plato's Symposium*

Stanley Rosen, *Plato's Sophist: The Drama of Original and Image*

Stanley Rosen, *Plato's Statesman*

Seth Benardete, *Herodotean Inquiries*

Seth Benardete, *Achilles and Hector: The Homeric Hero*

Seth Benardete, *Sacred Transgressions: A Reading of Sophocles' Angigone*

Henrik Syse, *Natural Law, Religion, and Rights*

Jacques Maritain, *Natural Law: Reflections on Theory and Practice*

Ronna Burger, *The Phaedo: A Platonic Labyrinth*

Joseph Cropsey, *Polity and Economy: With Further Thoughts on the Principles of Adam Smith*

Ian S. Ross, ed., *On the Wealth of Nations: Contemporary Responses to Adam Smith*

G.A.J. Rogers, ed., *Leviathan: Contemporary Responses to the Political Theory of Thomas Hobbes*

Bosanquet, Bernard, *The Philosophical Theory of the State and Related Issues*

Leszek Kolakowski, *My Correct Views on Everything*

Xenophon's Socratic Discourse
An Intepretation of the *Oeconomicus*

Leo Strauss

With a new, literal translation of the
Oeconomicus by Carnes Lord

Foreword by Christopher Bruell

ST. AUGUSTINE'S PRESS
South Bend, Indiana

Manufactured in the United States of America

1 2 3 4 5 6   11 10 09 08 07 06 05 04

Cataloging in Publication Data

Strauss, Leo.
    Xenophon's Socratic discourse: an interpretation of the
    Oeconomicus / by Leo Strauss: with a new, literal
    translation of the Oeconomicus by Carnes Lord
       p.   cm.
    Includes bibliographical references and index.
    ISBN 1-890318-96-5 (cloth: alk. paper)
    1. Economics—Greece—History. 2. Administration of
    estates—Greece—Historiography. 3. Xenophon.
    Oeconomicus. 4. Greece—Economic conditions—
    Historiography. 5. Socrates. I. Xenophon. Oeconomicus.
    English. II. Lord, Carnes. III. Title.
    HB108.A2S73 1997
    330.15'12—dc21   97-37672
                                                            CIP

Paperback edition ISBN: 1-58731-966-7

∞ The paper used in this publication meets the minimum requirements of
the American National Standard for Information Sciences—Permanence
of Paper for Printed Materials, ANSI Z39.4888–1984.

Preface

After a silence of more than twenty years on the subject, Leo Strauss has returned to the study of Xenophon, demonstrating his contention that this now neglected and despised author is one of the most important sources for the undertanding of political things. His influential earlier work *On Tyranny* (republished by Cornell University Press in 1968) deals with a dialogue (the *Hiero*) in which Socrates does not appear. That work implies that the Socratic side of Xenophon's thought needs complementary treatment, and it is to his explicit presentation of Socrates that this interpretation is devoted. It is a major contribution to the undersanding of the authentic Socratic teaching, and hence capital for our knowledge of the origin and meaning of political science as well as its relation to political practice. This dialogue provides a portrait of the philosopher in his delicate relation to his fellow men.

A new, literal translation of the *Oeconomicus* by Carnes Lord is included to enable the reader to follow Professor Strauss's careful and subtle treatment of the text. It is to a rediscovery of that text as a source of knowledge and inspiration that Professor Strauss's great scholarship is dedicated; and this implies a respect, hardly dominant today, for the text as it was written by its author. It is our hope that this volume will serve as a model for the reading of the classical literature.

ALLAN BLOOM

Paris
February 1970

Contents

Foreword by Christopher Bruell   ix

The *Oeconomicus*, by Xenophon   1

Xenophon's Socratic Discourse, by Leo Strauss   81

Introduction   81

The title and the opening   83

A definition of household management (Chapter I)   87

The turn to the examination of Kritoboulos and
     Socrates (Chapter II)   100

Socrates' promises (Chapter III)   107

The case for farming—I (Chapter IV)   113

The case for farming—II (Chapter V)   120

A simplifying retrospect and a complicating prospect
     (Chapter VI)   125

Gynaikologia—I: Marriage according to the gods and
     according to the law (Chapter VII)   131

Gynaikologia—II: Order, I (Chapter VIII)   140

Gynaikologia—III: Order, II (Chapter IX)   146

Gynaikologia—IV: Cosmetics (Chapter X)   153

Andrologia (Chapter XI)   159

How to educate stewards to good will and diligence
     (Chapter XII)   167

How to educate stewards to rulership (Chapter XIII)   171

How to educate stewards to justice (Chapter XIV)   174

Transition to the art of farming (Chapter XI)   178

The nature of the land the the proper beginning of the
account of farming (Chapter XVI)   182

Sowing as well as reaping, threshing, and winnowing
(Chapters XVII–XVIII)   187

Planting (Chapter XIX)   193

The art of farming and love of farming (Chapter XX)   197

The art of farming and the kingly man (Chapter XXI)   205

Index   211

Foreword

The publication by St. Augustine's Press of paperback editions of Leo Strauss's last two books on Xenophon, the last two books which he published in his lifetime, presents to a new generation of students works that have already perplexed more than one generation of readers since their first appearance in the early 1970s. It was to be expected that they would make extreme demands on their readers' seriousness, as well as on their alertness and concentration, their patience and perseverance: all of Strauss's writings do that. But even readers already familiar with his work, or especially such readers, are often surprised, not to say disconcerted, at encountering a reserve or economy of expression remarkable even for him, together with a lightness of tone which, if not unprecedented in his earlier writing, appears to be more pervasive than hitherto. One is all the more surprised, therefore, to discover from a letter written in the last year of his life to a scholar whom he held in the highest regard that Strauss himself considered these books to be his best works: "I am glad that you received my two books on Xenophon's Socrates. They are not the last thing I have written, but I believe they are the best and part of it may be of interest to you. They develop at some length, if not eo nomine, what I indicated in *The City and Man* p. 61 regarding the difference between Socrates and The Bible."[1] Yet as this also suggests,

---

[1] Letter to Gershom Scholem of 11/17/72; cf. letter of 9/6/72 to the same correspondent. Leo Strauss, *Gesammelte Schriften*, vol. 3, ed. Heinrich and Wiebke Meier (Stuttgart/Weimar: J. B. Metzler 2001), pp. 764–65 and 762.

a consideration of what Strauss can have meant by the judgment of his books that he expressed to Scholem may facili-
tate our access to them—by casting some light on the puz-
zling features already noted, if not also in other ways.

Let us see, then, whether what the two books themselves
reveal to us about their character and intention makes intel-
ligible such a judgment. They treat between them the four
Socratic writings of Xenophon. The second of the books,
Xenophon's Socrates, which treats three of these writings
including the longest, has no "Introduction" but only a very
brief "Preface." (The "Preface" calls attention to the fact that
Strauss has repeated in the book "some points" which he
"had been compelled to make in the earlier publication." He
excuses himself to "the reader who notices the repetitions":
one can infer that Strauss addresses himself to such readers
and alerts them in the "Preface" to the fact that the second
book will confirm the first in some significant respect or
respects. This is only fitting, since he had devoted the first
book to that one of Xenophon's Socratic writings which
seemed to him "the most revealing and at the same time the
most misunderstood.") By failing to supply the second book
with an "Introduction," Strauss brought it about that the
"Introduction" to the first, *Xenophon's Socratic Discourse*,
serves as introduction to the whole constituted by the two
volumes taken together. But that "Introduction" is itself
rather brief, and the task of announcing the theme of the
books is assigned to only one of its eight paragraphs. (The
seven others are devoted to showing why someone concerned with that theme might reasonably turn to Xenophon
and to distinguishing his four Socratic writings from one
another, by way of indicating the particular character and
significance of the one that the first book is to treat.) This
paragraph, with which indeed the book opens, reads as follows:

> The Great Tradition of political philosophy was orig-
> inated by Socrates.
> Socrates is said to have disregarded the whole
> of nature altogether in order to devote himself
> entirely to the study of ethical things. His reason
> seems to have been that while man is not neces-
> sarily in need of knowledge of the nature of all
> things, he must of necessity be concerned with
> how he should live individually and collectively.

The singularity of this paragraph as an introduction to a
work or works of Strauss can be properly gauged only by a
thorough comparison with the ways in which he introduced
each of his other books. For present purposes, however, it
may suffice to cast a glance at the "Introduction" to the volume which stands closest to the two Xenophon books in
spirit and theme, if not also in time. (It stands closest in time,
if one considers only books written originally as books and
excludes collections of essays.) The first paragraph of the
"Introduction" to *Socrates and Aristophanes* reads as follows:

> Our Great Tradition includes political philosophy and
> thus seems to vouch for its possibility and necessity.
> According to the same tradition, political philosophy
> was founded by Socrates.

In comparing these two first paragraphs, we are struck at
once by their similarity—and only thereafter by a profound
difference. In the introduction to the Xenophon volumes,
Strauss no longer seeks an extrinsic warrant (in tradition or
elsewhere) for the "possibility and necessity" of political
philosophy. Nor does he offer a justification for returning to
the origin of political philosophy, that is, to Socrates, as he
had done a bit further on in the earlier introduction:

> The problem of Socrates as we have sketched it . . . can

only be preparatory to "the problem of Socrates" as stated by Nietzsche: The question of what Socrates stood for inevitably becomes the question of the worth of what Socrates stood for. In other words, the return to the origins of the Great Tradition has become necessary because of the radical questioning of that tradition. . . .

The counterpart, in the Xenophon introduction, to those lines is a remark which Strauss makes almost in passing:

Our age boasts of being more open to everything human than any earlier age; it is surely blind to the greatness of Xenophon. Without intending it, one might make some discoveries about our age by reading and rereading Xenophon.

Here, in other words, it is not Socrates or political philosophy that is called before the bar (a bar belonging to, if not constituted by, "our age"); it is rather "our age" about which one could (from a perspective to be unfolded in the works before one) reach a fitting judgment, provided that one would still be concerned to do so. And by departing in this way from his practice of justifying his studies by appeals to concerns rooted in our particular situation, a practice that had still left its traces even on *Socrates and Aristophanes*, Strauss indicates that he has gone further in his books on Xenophon's Socrates than he had ever permitted himself to do before—for Strauss, too, "refused to separate from one another wisdom and moderation" (*Xenophon's Socrates* p. 78)—in presenting what he regards as the highest subject matter as it appears in (or to) itself.

But in describing these books as his best works, Strauss must have thought not merely of their subject matter and point of view but also of the manner of its treatment. What, then, is the necessary or appropriate manner for presenting, so far as possible, the philosophic life as it appears in and to itself? Since Strauss chose to tackle this task by way of a treatment of Xenophon's Socrates, we can assume that he regarded Xenophon and his Socrates as models also in this respect. After noting, therefore, that Xenophon has Socrates refer to certain "'physiological' questions"—that is, to questions belonging to the sphere of Socrates' "main concern" (*Xenophon's Socrates* p. 8)—at "an advanced stage of a drinking party where a greater *parrhesia* [outspokenness] is in order than elsewhere," Strauss comments: "The 'physiological' part of his [Socrates'] wisdom, nay, his whole wisdom can be shown without disguise only 'in fun'; so close is the connection between wisdom and laughter." (*Xenophon's Socrates* p. 170; cf. p. 92) Noting, on another occasion, that Xenophon has Socrates explain a remark of his only after an intelligent question or objection has been put to him, Strauss comments: "To state clearly what he means, he must apparently be sure that the one to whom he talks does some thinking." (*Xenophon's Socrates* p. 82; cf. p. 122) For our present purpose, this comment appears to create a greater difficulty than the preceding one: a writer, too, can express himself light-heartedly, not to say jocularly, but can he respond to his reader's questions or objections? Yes, if the same remark can mean one thing to someone who merely "takes it in" but quite another to one who, following the implicit argument on his own, puts to it at each stage the correct questions.

I will add two remarks which, at or about the time when he was writing these books, Strauss made to a young student of his acquaintance. Regarding *Xenophon's Socratic Discourse*, he said, while he was still working on it, that it is "the first book in which I address myself solely to an intelligent younger man *monos pros monon* [one alone to one alone]." Sometime after the completion of *Xenophon's Socrates*, he was asked by the student about its strange beginning and equally strange ending. (The beginning calls attention to the derivation from a verb that can mean "remembering one's grudge" of the term used for the title of the longest of the Socratic writings; the ending appears to go out of its way to associate Xenophon himself with a character of his who was a critic of Socrates.) Strauss replied: "As for Xenophon's possible critique of Socrates, it is ironical: he resented his corruption." It is safe to assume that what was true of Xenophon vis-à-vis Socrates was true also of Strauss: that he, too, "resented" his corruption at the hands of Socrates (and others) and therefore made such corruption *the* theme of his last two Xenophon books. (Compare *Xenophon's Socrates* p. 171 toward the bottom.)

As this suggests, to the right kind of reader Strauss presents in these books, as in no other books of his, also himself: himself as he truly was, *monos pros monon*. For that reader will be one who, awake to each remark of Strauss (who mentions something if he has noticed that it is important), continues to look in the direction pointed out to him until he has seen what Strauss, too, saw. And, seeing it (what Strauss saw, as he saw it), he draws close to, comes to know, not only the subject matter but also the make of the man who has helped to guide him toward it.

A Note on the Texts Treated in the Two Books

In seeking indication of the overall view of Xenophon's Socratic writings by which Strauss took his bearings in his treatment of each one of them, we must not lose sight of the singleness of purpose uniting his two books. As an additional example of their unity, we might mention the facts that the "Introduction" and therewith the first book altogether all but begins with a reference to the "powerful prejudice which emerged in the course of the nineteenth century and is today firmly established" according to which "Xenophon is so simple-minded and narrow-minded or philistine that he cannot have grasped the core or depth of Socrates' thought"; whereas the second book confides its last word to an "Appendix" which locates the "most telling" manifestation of such prejudice in a certain nineteenth century German scholar and goes on to indicate how the specific limitation of that scholar (which made him "blind to the greatness of Xenophon") would have looked from Xenophon's own point of view. It can no longer be surprising therefore that, while it is the "Introduction" that provides a synoptic account of the three texts treated in the second book, it is left to the "Preface" to supply a piece of information necessary to a full appreciation of the importance that Strauss attached to the single text which he treated in the first.

The longest of Xenophon's Socratic writings is the one whose title is usually rendered as Memorabilia (Recollections). As Strauss makes clear in the "Introduction," Xenophon (a man famous in his own right, who had "accomplished some deeds and pronounced some speeches which he considered worth remembering") devoted "his recollections par excellence" rather to what he remembered of his teacher, Socrates. More precisely, he devoted those recollections to establishing Socrates' justice, since the first or shorter part of the text in question is devoted to showing that Socrates was innocent of the charges on which he was convicted by an Athenian jury and put to death, while the second or longer part is devoted to showing how Socrates benefited his companions (and others). This means, according to Strauss, that the other three Socratic writings "are devoted to Socrates *tout court* or to Socrates even if he transcends justice." It is one of these that Strauss chose to treat in the first book. Which one and why? As he explains, the three texts which treat Socrates *tout court* divide the task among themselves. The *Symposium* is devoted to Socrates' deed or deeds; the *Apology of Socrates to the Jury* to his deliberating; and the *Oeconomicus*, the text chosen for treatment in the first book, to his speaking or conversing. According to the

"Introduction," the reason would seem to be that the *Oeconomicus* is "Xenophon's Socratic *logos* or discourse par excellence." To this reason, the "Preface" adds that "in its central chapter Socrates is directly contrasted with a perfect gentleman" (that is, a man who embodies the virtues treated in Books III–V of Aristotle's *Nicomachean Ethics*, for example, or those about which Socrates was always inquiring according to *Memorabilia* I.1.16). The two reasons are linked. The contrast between Socrates and the perfect gentleman was of paramount interest to Socrates himself: it was to learn about a gentleman's virtue that Socrates sought one out. (*Oeconomicus* VI–VII and XI) And it was the conversation to which that initiative on his part led that was the "Socratic *logos* or discourse par excellence."

Two of Xenophon's Socratic writings, the *Symposium* and the *Apology of Socrates to the Jury*, have a namesake (or near namesake) among the Platonic dialogues. Xenophon's *Symposium*, too, presents Socrates at a dinner/drinking party. The host is not the poet Agathon but rather a wealthy Athenian gentleman by the name of Kallias; and eros is only one among a number of themes discussed. (Kallias is a Platonic character, as well: the host of the gathering portrayed in the *Protagoras* at which, curiously enough, almost all of the participants in Plato's *Symposium* are also present.) Xenophon's *Apology of Socrates*, unlike Plato's, gives only excerpts from the speeches made by Socrates at his trial; on the other hand, it presents the reasoning (deliberation) that led him to conduct his defense in the provocative manner in which he did. Socrates' trial is treated by Xenophon also in the *Memorabilia*. (I.1–2 and IV.8) There he presents, as Plato did not, a number of the remarks that had been made by Socrates' accusers. (I.2) Strauss's summary orientation implies—what his books also show—that despite these and other differences of presentation (see further *Xenophon's Socrates* pp. 53 and 83, for example, as well as *Xenophon's*

Socratic Discourse p. 164) Xenophon's Socrates is identical to the Socrates of the Platonic dialogues.

CHRISTOPHER BRUELL

Suggestions for Further Reading

A. Translations of Xenophon's Socratic Writings

1. *Memorabilia*, translated and annotated by Amy L. Bonnette (Ithaca: Cornell University Press 1994).

2. *The Shorter Socratic Writings (Apology of Socrates to the Jury, Oeconomicus, and Symposium)*, edited by Robert C. Bartlett (Ithaca: Cornell University Press 1996).

B. Other Writings of Leo Strauss on Xenophon

1. "The Spirit of Sparta or the Taste of Xenophon," *Social Research* VI:4, pp. 502–36.

2. *On Tyranny*, edited by Victor Gourevitch and Michael S. Roth (Chicago: The University of Chicago Press 2000).

3. "The Origins of Political Science and the Problem of Socrates: Six Public Lectures," *Interpretation* XXIII:2, pp. 158–78.

4. "Greek Historians," *The Review of Metaphysics* XXI, pp. 656–66.

5. "Xenophon's *Anabasis*," *Studies in Platonic Political Philosophy* (Chicago: The University of Chicago Press 1983), pp. 105–36.

C. Discussions of Strauss's Works on Xenophon

1. "Philosophy and Politics I–II," by Victor Gourevitch, *The Review of Metaphysics* XXII, pp. 58–84 and 281–328.
2. "Strauss on Xenophon's Socrates," by Christopher Bruell, *The Political Science Reviewer*, XIV, pp. 263–318.

The *Oeconomicus*

by XENOPHON

I

(1) I once heard him discourse on the management of the household as well, in about these words.[1]

"Tell me, Kritoboulos," he said, "is management of the household the name of a certain kind of knowledge, as medicine, smithing, and carpentry are?"

"It seems so to me, at least," said Kritoboulos.

(2) "Then just as we are at no loss to say what the work of each of these arts is, can we also say what the work of household management is?"

"It seems, at any rate," said Kritoboulos, "that it is the part of a good household manager to manage his own household well."

(3) "But if someone were to entrust another's household to him," said Socrates, "could he not manage that, if he wanted to, as well as he does his own? For the one who knows carpentry can do equally for another what he does for himself; and so too, presumably, can the skilled household manager."

"It seems so to me, at least, Socrates."

(4) "Is it possible, then," said Socrates, "for one who knows

[1] The translation has been made, by permission of the Clarendon Press, Oxford, from the Oxford Classical Text, *Xenophontis Opera Omnia*, II (2d ed.; Oxford: Clarendon Press, 1921), edited by E. C. Marchant. All deviations from the readings of that text are specifically noted. The *oikonomikos* is the "skilled household manager," not merely the "household manager" (*oikonomos*) mentioned in I.2 and I.15. For a discussion of the significance of Xenophon's titles see Leo Strauss, *On Tyranny* (Ithaca, N.Y.: Cornell University Press, 1968), pp. 30–34.

this art, even though he happens to have no wealth himself, to manage another's household, just as a builder can build another's house, and earn pay for it?"

"Yes, by Zeus, and he would earn a lot of pay," said Kritoboulos, "if on taking over, he were able to do what's necessary and, in producing a surplus, increase the household."

(5) "But what in our opinion is a household? Is it just the house, or is whatever one possesses outside the house also part of the household?"

"To me, at any rate," said Kritoboulos, "it seems that whatever someone possesses is part of his household, even if it isn't in the same city as the possessor."

(6) "Don't some men possess enemies?"

"Yes, by Zeus; and some, at least, have a great many."

"Shall we say the enemies are also their possessions?"

"But it would be ridiculous," said Kritoboulos, "if the one who increases enemies should in addition earn pay for it."

(7) "Because, of course, it was our opinion that a man's household is whatever he possesses."

"Yes, by Zeus," said Kritoboulos, "at least if what he possesses is good; for whatever is bad, by Zeus, I do not call a possession."

"You, then, appear to call possessions whatever is beneficial to each."

"Very much so," he said, "and whatever is harmful I hold to be loss rather than wealth."

(8) "If, therefore, someone buys a horse he doesn't know how to use and hurts himself in a fall, the horse isn't wealth for him?" [2]

"No, at least if wealth is a good."

[2] Etymologically, *chrēsthai* ("to use") is related to *chrēma* ("wealth") as *ktasthai* ("to possess") is related to *ktēma* ("possession").

"Then not even the earth is wealth for the human being who works it in such a way as to suffer loss in working it."

"No, the earth isn't wealth either, if it brings hardship instead of nourishment."

(9) "And isn't it the same with sheep: if someone suffers loss through not knowing how to use them, the sheep aren't wealth for him?"

"It seems so to me, at least."

"You, then, as it appears, believe that whatever benefits is wealth, while whatever harms is not."

"Just so."

(10) "Then the same things are wealth for the one knowing how to use each of them and not wealth for the one not knowing how; just as flutes are wealth for the one knowing how to play the flute in a manner worth mentioning, while for the one not knowing how they are nothing more than useless stones, as long as he doesn't sell them. (11) And thus it looks to us as though the flutes are wealth for those not knowing how to use them only when they sell them, and not when they don't sell them but keep them in their possession."

"Neither of us can disagree with this argument, Socrates, since it was said that whatever is beneficial is wealth. So unsold flutes are not wealth, for they aren't useful, but sold ones are wealth."

(12) To this Socrates said: "At least, if he knows how to sell. For should he sell them and in turn receive something he didn't know how to use, they wouldn't be wealth even when sold, at least according to your argument."

"You appear to be saying, Socrates, that not even money is wealth if one doesn't know how to use it."

(13) "And you seem to me to agree that whatever can benefit someone is wealth. Well, what if someone were to use his

money to buy a prostitute, and through her he became worse in body, worse in soul, and worse in regard to his household—in what way would the money still be beneficial to him?"

"In no way, unless, of course, we are going to say that the so-called pig bean,[3] which brings madness to all who eat of it, is wealth."

(14) "Then unless one knows how to use money, let him thrust it so far away, Kritoboulos, that it isn't even wealth. As for friends, if one knows how to use them so as to be benefited by them, what shall we assert they are?"

"Wealth, by Zeus," said Kritoboulos, "and worth much more than oxen, if indeed they are more beneficial than oxen."

(15) "Then enemies too are wealth, at least according to your argument, for whoever is able to benefit from them."

"It seems so to me, at any rate."

"It is the part of a good household manager, therefore, to know how to use enemies so as to benefit from enemies."

"Most emphatically."

"And of course you see, Kritoboulos," he said, "how many households of private men have been increased through war, and how many through tyrannies."[4]

(16) "These things seem to me finely spoken, Socrates," said Kritoboulos; "but what does it look like to us when we see some who have both the kinds of knowledge and the resources which they might put to work to increase their house-

---

[3] "Pig bean" is a literal translation of *byoskyamos* ("henbane").

[4] A translation of the Oxford text of this sentence reads: "how many households of private men have been increased through war, and how many of tyrants." This alteration seems warranted neither by the evidence of the manuscripts nor by the sense of the passage. At most, one might change *tyranniōn* ("tyrannies") to *tyrannōn* ("tyrants"). In any case, the contrast is not between tyrants and private men, which would not be in point here, but between two situations in which private men "benefit from enemies."

holds, and we perceive that they're unwilling to do it, and see that as a result their knowledge is of no benefit to them? What else than that for them the kinds of knowledge are not wealth, and neither are the possessions?"

(17) "Is it slaves, Kritoboulos," said Socrates, "you are attempting to discuss with me?"

"No, by Zeus," he said, "not I, but rather men of whom some at least are reputed to be very wellborn; some of these I see have the kinds of knowledge that belong to war, others those that belong to peace, yet they are unwilling to put them to work—I suppose for this reason, that they do not have masters."

(18) "And how is it they have no masters," said Socrates, "if in spite of the fact that they pray for happiness and want to do the things from which good will result for them, they are nevertheless prevented from doing so by the rulers?"

"And just who are these invisible rulers of theirs?" said Kritoboulos.

(19) "But by Zeus," said Socrates, "they are not invisible at all, but rather quite manifest. And surely it doesn't escape your notice that they are most wicked, that is, if you hold that inactivity and softness of soul and neglect are wicked. (20) And there are other deceiving mistresses, pretending to be pleasures —dice-playing and human associations without benefit—which in time become obvious even to the deceived as pains with a mere gloss of pleasure, and which, when they are in control, keep men from beneficial works."

(21) "But others, Socrates," he said, "are not prevented from working by these things; on the contrary, they apply themselves quite vigorously to their work and to devising means of income, and yet at the same time they deplete the households and are continually without means."

(22) "These too are slaves," said Socrates, "and slaves indeed to harsh masters, some to gluttony, some to lust, some to drunkenness, some to foolish and expensive ambitions—all of which rule the human beings they control so harshly as to compel them, while they see them in their prime and capable of working, to spend on their desires whatever they may gain from their work; and when their masters perceive that they are no longer capable of working due to age, they abandon them to grow old miserably and attempt to use others in turn as slaves. (23) It is no less necessary, Kritoboulos, to fight for freedom against them than against those who attempt to enslave by arms. Enemies, when they are gentlemen and have enslaved others, have in fact compelled many to become better by moderating them and have made them live in greater ease in the time remaining to them; but these mistresses never cease to plague the bodies, the souls, and the households of human beings as long as they rule over them."

II

(1) Thereupon Kritoboulos spoke somewhat as follows. "As regards such things, it seems to me I've heard enough of your sayings. On examining myself I seem to find I am fairly self-controlled in such matters, so that if you advise me about what I might do to increase my household, it seems to me I wouldn't be prevented from doing it, at least by those things you call mistresses. Be confident, then, and give me your good advice; or do you charge us, Socrates, with being sufficiently rich already, and do we seem to you to need no additional wealth?"

(2) "Not I," said Socrates. "But if you're speaking of me as well, I seem to need no additional wealth and indeed to be sufficiently rich; but you, Kritoboulos, you seem to me to be

very poor, and, yes, by Zeus, there are times when I greatly pity you."

(3) And Kritoboulos spoke, laughing. "And how much—by the gods—do you, Socrates," he said, "suppose your possessions would bring if they were sold, and how much mine?"

"I suppose," said Socrates, "that my house and all my substance [5] would quite easily bring five minas, if I chanced on a good buyer; but I know with some accuracy that your things would bring more than a hundred times that."

(4) "And though you understand this, you still believe you need no additional wealth, while you pity me for my poverty?"

"My things are sufficient to provide enough for me," he said, "but with the pomp you have assumed and your reputation, even if you had three times what you possess now, it seems to me it wouldn't be sufficient for you."

(5) "How so?" said Kritoboulos.

Socrates declared: "First, because I see you are compelled to make frequent and great sacrifices, as otherwise, I suppose, neither gods nor human beings could put up with you; then, because it's appropriate for you to receive many foreigners, and to do so with magnificence; and then, because you must feast the citizens and treat them well, or be bereft of allies. (6) And again I perceive that the city orders you to accomplish great things—breeding of horses and training of choruses, support of the gymnasia, public commands; and if war should come, I know they will order you to support a trireme and to contribute so much that you will be hard put to sustain it. And should you seem to have performed some one of these things

[5] *Ta onta,* literally, "the beings" or "the things that are." The translation "substance" attempts to preserve this larger sense of the expression in a context where it means "possessions" or "goods."

inadequately, I know the Athenians will punish you no less than they would if they caught you stealing something of theirs. (7) In addition I see that you, supposing yourself to be rich and therefore neglecting to devise means to wealth, apply your thought to boyish affairs, as though that were possible for you. For these reasons I pity you, lest you suffer some irreparable evil and end up in the worst poverty. (8) As for me, if I need anything more for myself, I know you too understand that there are some who would help me and who could, by supplying a very little, overwhelm my way of life with a deluge of abundance; but your friends, though what they have is more sufficient for their condition than what you have is for yours, nevertheless look to you as a source of benefits."

(9) And Kritoboulos spoke. "To these things, Socrates, I have no response; rather it's time for you to take command of me, before I become really pitiable."

After having heard this, Socrates spoke. "And doesn't it seem a wonderful thing you are doing, Kritoboulos—that you should have laughed at me a little while ago when I asserted I was rich, as though I didn't know what a rich man was, and then not given up until you had refuted me and made me admit to possessing not the hundredth part of your things, while now you bid me take command of you and make it my concern [6] that you don't become altogether and in truth a poor man?"

---

[6] This is the first occurrence in the dialogue of the verb *epimeleisthai*, meaning, roughly, "to be concerned with," "to take care that," "to be careful," "to be diligent." The verb as well as the noun derived from it, *epimeleia*, become thematic in Chapter XII. Wherever possible these terms are translated, respectively, "to be diligent" and "diligence"; otherwise, "to be concerned" or "to concern oneself," and "concern." The related terms *amelein* and *ameleia* are rendered, respectively, "to neglect" or "to be negligent," and "neglect."

(10) "It's because I see, Socrates," he said, "that you know one enriching work: how to produce a surplus. I expect that one who saves something from a little could very easily produce a large surplus from much."

(11) "Don't you remember, then, what you were saying a moment ago in the argument—when you wouldn't permit me to utter a sound—that horses wouldn't be wealth for the one not knowing how to use them, and neither would the earth nor sheep nor money nor any single thing that one didn't know how to use? It's from such things that income derives; yet how do you suppose I will know how to use any one of them when I've never had the rule over them?"

(12) "But it seemed to us that, even if someone happened to have no wealth of his own, there could still be a knowledge of household management. What then prevents you from knowing as well?"

"The very thing, by Zeus, that would prevent a human being from knowing how to play the flute, that is, if he had never possessed flutes himself and another had never made provision for him to learn on his. This is just my situation in regard to household management. (13) For I myself have never possessed the instrument—wealth—with which to learn, nor has another ever provided me with his own to manage, except for you who are now willing to provide yours. But, surely, those who are just learning to play the lyre usually ruin the lyres; if I were to undertake to learn household management in your household, I would perhaps utterly ruin it for you."

(14) To this Kritoboulos said: "At any rate you're trying eagerly, Socrates, to avoid being of any benefit to me in carrying on more easily my necessary affairs."

"No, by Zeus," said Socrates, "not at all; on the contrary, I shall very eagerly explain to you whatever I know. (15) But

I suppose if you had come for fire and I had none, you wouldn't blame me if I led you to some other place where you could get it; and if you asked me for water and I, having none myself, took you to some other place and took you to it, I know you wouldn't blame me for that either; and if you wished to learn music from me, and I pointed out to you some who were much cleverer in music than I and would be grateful if you were willing to learn from them, how, again, could you blame me for doing this?"

(16) "I couldn't justly blame you, Socrates."

"Then I'll point out to you, Kritoboulos, certain others who are much cleverer than I in those things you persist in wanting to learn from me. I admit I have been diligent in finding those in the city who are the most knowledgeable in each kind of thing. (17) For on learning that among those who are in the same line of work some were very poor and others very rich, I wondered greatly, and it seemed worthwhile to investigate why this should be. On investigating it, I found that these things happen quite properly. (18) I saw those who act at random suffering loss, and I noticed that those who are diligent and apply their minds do things more quickly, more easily, and more profitably. From these, I suppose, you too could learn, if you wanted to and the god did not oppose you, how to become an extremely clever money-maker."

III

(1) After having heard this, Kritoboulos spoke. "Now then," he said, "I won't let you go, Socrates, until you have shown what you promised in the presence of these friends here."

"What, then, Kritoboulos," said Socrates, "if I first show you, with respect to houses, some who build useless ones for a great deal of money, and others who for much less build ones that have everything that's necessary—will I seem to display [7] to you one of the works of household management?"

"Very much so," said Kritoboulos.

(2) "And what if after this, and following on this, I display to you some who possess very many belongings of every sort and yet don't have them for use when they need them and don't even know when they're secure, and who as a result are themselves greatly harassed and harass the servants in turn, and others who possess no more, but even less, yet have them always ready for use when they need them?"

(3) "Is anything else the cause of this, Socrates, than that for the first everything is thrown down by chance, while for the others each kind of thing is kept in order in a place?"

"Yes, by Zeus," said Socrates, "and not in just any chance place; rather, wherever it's appropriate, there each kind of thing is ordered separately."

"In speaking of this, also," said Kritoboulos, "you seem to me to be talking about a part of household management." [8]

(4) "What, then," he said, "if I display to you, in respect to servants, certain places where all of them are tied down, so to speak, and yet frequently run away, and others where they are released and yet are willing to work and to remain—won't I seem to display to you a work of household management that is worth looking at?"

"Yes, by Zeus," said Kritoboulos, "certainly."

(5) "And also, in respect to those who farm very similar

[7] "Display" translates *epideiknunai*; "show," *apodeiknunai*. The latter term conveys a suggestion of demonstrative proof; the former, of rhetorical virtuosity. Both are compounds of *deiknunai*, "point out," which first occurs in II.15–16.

[8] The expression *tōn oikonomikōn* here and in III.1 could also mean "of those skilled in household management."

farms, some claiming they have been destroyed by farming who in fact are very poor, and others having all they need from farming in fine and abundant supply?"

"Yes, by Zeus," said Kritoboulos. "For perhaps they squander, spending not only on what's necessary but also on what brings harm to themselves and the household."

(6) "Perhaps there are some like this," said Socrates. "But I'm speaking not of them but rather of those who have nothing even for the necessary expenses, though they claim to be farmers."

"And what would be the cause of this, Socrates?"

"I'll take you to them as well," said Socrates; "by looking you'll surely learn it."

"By Zeus," he said, "at least if I'm able."

(7) "In looking you must test yourself, to see whether you can understand. Now I've known you to get up very early in the morning and go a very long way on foot to look at comedies and eagerly persuade me to join in the looking; but not once did you ever invite me to this other kind of work."

"I must look ridiculous to you, Socrates."

(8) "But far more ridiculous to yourself, by Zeus," he said. "And what if I display to you some who, through horsemanship, have been brought to poverty as regards even the necessary things, and others who are very well off through horsemanship and take pride in the profit?"

"I too see such people and I know both sorts, yet I do not any more on that account become one of those who profit."

(9) "That's because you look at them as you look at tragedies and comedies—not, I suppose, in order to become a poet, but rather that you may take pleasure in seeing or hearing something. And perhaps it's right this way, as you don't want to become a poet; but since you are compelled to make use of horsemanship, don't you suppose you would be a fool not to

consider how you might avoid being merely a layman [9] in this work, especially as the same horses are both good for using and profitable for selling?"

(10) "Is it colt-breaking [10] you suggest I do, Socrates?"

"No, by Zeus, no more than I suggest you buy children and equip them to be farmers; but it seems to me there are certain ages at which both horses and human beings are immediately useful as well as susceptible to improvement. I can also display some who use the women they marry in such a way as to have them as co-workers in increasing the households, and others in a way that for the most part ruins them."

(11) "Must one fault the man or the woman [11] for this, Socrates?"

"When sheep fare badly," said Socrates, "we usually fault the shepherd, and when a horse behaves badly, we usually speak badly of the horseman; as for the woman, if she has been taught the good things by the man and still acts badly, the woman could perhaps justly be held at fault; on the other hand, if he doesn't teach the fine and good things but makes use of her though she is quite ignorant of them, wouldn't the man justly be held at fault? (12) In any event, speak the whole truth to us, Kritoboulos," he said, "for you are in the presence of friends. Is there anyone to whom you entrust more serious matters than to your wife?"

"No one," he said.

---

[9] *Idiōtēs,* a private individual as opposed to a public figure (cf. I.15); hence, an unskilled person as opposed to an expert.

[10] There is a play in Greek on the words for "colt-breaking" (*pōlo-damnein*) and "selling" (*pōlēsis*).

[11] *Anēr* and *gynē,* in this as in other contexts, mean also or primarily "husband" and "wife." Wherever possible *anēr* is translated "man"; it signifies the male in the emphatic sense, the "real man" as opposed to the ordinary "human being" (*anthrōpos*). See Strauss, *op. cit.,* p. 115, n. 35.

"And is there anyone with whom you discuss fewer things than your wife?"

"There aren't many, in any case," he said.

(13) "Did you marry her when she was a very young girl and had seen and heard as little as possible?"

"Yes, indeed."

"Then it's even more wonderful if she knows anything of what she ought to say or do than if she goes wrong."

(14) "Those who you say have good wives, Socrates—did they themselves educate them?"

"There's nothing like investigating the matter. I'll introduce you to Aspasia,[12] who will display all these things to you more knowledgeably than I. (15) But I hold that a woman who is a good partner in the household is a proper counterweight to the man in attaining the good. For while the possessions usually come into the house through the man's actions, they are expended for the most part in the course of the woman's housekeeping; and when these things turn out well, the households increase, but when done badly, the households diminish. (16) And I suppose I could also display to you those who put to work, in a manner worth mentioning, each of the other kinds of knowledge, if you hold that something further is needed."

IV

(1) "But why must you display all of them, Socrates?" said Kritoboulos. "It's not easy to get possession of the kinds of workers that are necessary in all the arts; nor is it possible to become experienced in all of them; but the kinds of knowledge that are reputed to be the finest and would be especially suita-

[12] The famous courtesan and mistress of Pericles, noted for her intellectual attainments.

ble for my concern—these you must display for me, as well as those who practice them, and you yourself must do what you can to benefit me in these matters by teaching me."

(2) "You speak finely, Kritoboulos," he said. "For indeed those that are called mechanical are spoken against everywhere and have quite plausibly come by a very bad reputation in the cities. For they utterly ruin the bodies of those who work at them and those who are concerned with them,[13] compelling them to sit still and remain indoors,[14] or in some cases even to spend the whole day by a fire. And when the bodies are made effeminate, the souls too become much more diseased. (3) Lack of leisure to join in the concerns of friends and of the city is another condition of those that are called mechanical; those who practice them are reputed to be bad friends as well as bad defenders of their fatherlands. Indeed in some of the cities, especially those reputed to be good at war, no citizen is allowed to work at the mechanical arts."

(4) "Then as for us, Socrates, which do you advise we make use of?"

"Should we be ashamed," said Socrates, "to imitate the king of Persia? For they say he believes farming and the art of war are among the finest and most necessary concerns, and concerns himself emphatically with both of them."

After having heard this, Kritoboulos spoke. (5) "Do you take this too on trust, Socrates," he said, "that the king of Persia concerns himself in some way with farming?"

"If we investigate the matter as follows, Kritoboulos," said Socrates, "perhaps we may learn whether in some way he does

[13] A distinction seems intended here between the workers and those who are merely "concerned" with the work, i.e., overseers of some kind. Cf. IV.10 and V.4.

[14] Literally, "to sit and nourish themselves with shadows."

concern himself with it. We agree he is emphatically concerned with the works of war, since it is he who gives orders to the rulers of however many nations send him tribute, regarding just how many horsemen and archers and slingers and targeteers each must maintain, that they may be sufficient both to control the ruled and to defend the country should enemies invade it. (6) Apart from these he maintains guards in the citadels, and the rulers are ordered in addition to provide maintenance for these garrisons. Every year the king holds an inspection of the mercenaries and the others he has ordered to be in arms, bringing together at various points of assembly all except those in the citadels. Those near his own residence he surveys himself; those further away he sends trusted officers to examine; (7) and whichever rulers of garrison and field troops [15] and the satraps look to have the full number as ordered and provide them equipped with splendid horses and arms, these rulers he increases with honors and enriches with great presents; but whichever rulers he finds have neglected the garrisons or looked to their own profit, these he punishes harshly and, removing them from rule, appoints others more diligent. In doing these things, then, it seems to us he is indisputably concerned with the works of war. (8) Again, whatever part of the country he rides through he surveys himself, and scrutinizes, and what he doesn't survey himself he examines by sending out trusted officers. And whichever rulers he perceives have provided that the country is well inhabited and that the earth is productive and replete with crops and with every kind of tree that it bears, these he enlarges with new territory,

---

[15] "Garrison commanders" (*phrourarchoi*) and "commanders of a thousand" (*chiliarchoi*); the latter term may also designate the ruler of a (Persian) military district. Xenophon goes on to suggest that these men are "rulers" (*archontes*) not only in name.

adorns with presents, and rewards with seats of honor; but whichever he sees have an inactive [16] country and few human beings, whether through harshness or arrogance or neglect, these he punishes and, removing them from rule, appoints other rulers. (9) In doing these things, then, does he seem any less concerned that the earth be made productive by its inhabitants than that it be well guarded by the garrisons? The rulers he has ordered to each thing are, furthermore, never the same, but certain ones rule the inhabitants and the workers and collect taxes from them, and certain others rule the armed garrisons.[17] (10) And if the ruler of the garrison doesn't sufficiently defend the country, the one who rules the inhabitants and is concerned with the works brings an accusation against him on the ground that the people cannot work because of the lack of a guard; but if the ruler of the garrison provides peace for the works, while the ruler provides but few human beings and an inactive country, then the ruler of the garrison brings an accusation against him. (11) For those who work the land badly will hardly be able either to maintain the garrisons or to pay taxes. But when a satrap is appointed, he concerns himself with both these things."

(12) Thereupon Kritoboulos spoke. "If the king indeed acts in this way, Socrates, it seems to me he concerns himself no less with the works of farming than with those of war."

(13) "But again, in addition to this," said Socrates, "in whatever countries the king resides, or wherever he travels, he is concerned that there be gardens, the so-called pleasure gardens,[18] filled with all the fine and good things that the earth

[16] *Argos,* "inactive" or "lazy" (in XV.2), is the opposite of *energos,* "productive"; both are related to the word for "work," *ergon.*

[17] In the Oxford text this phrase is emended to read, in translation: "both the armed [troops] and the garrisons."

[18] Xenophon uses the Persian word *paradeisoi.*

wishes to bring forth, and in these he himself spends most of his time, when the season of the year doesn't preclude it."

(14) "By Zeus," said Kritoboulos, "but it's a necessity, Socrates, that the king should concern himself that the place where he spends time be very finely equipped with trees and all the other fine things that the earth brings forth."

(15) "And some assert, Kritoboulos," said Socrates, "that when the king gives presents, he first sends for those who have proved themselves good in war, on the ground that there would be no benefit in plowing very much if there were no defenders; and that secondly he sends for those who cultivate their lands in the best manner and make them productive, saying that not even the brave could live if there were no workers. (16) It is also said that Cyrus, a king of the highest reputation, once told those who were called to receive presents that he himself should justly take the presents for both these things; for he was best, he said, both in cultivating the land and in protecting what was cultivated." [19]

(17) "Cyrus, at any rate," said Kritoboulos, "took no less pride, Socrates, in making his lands productive and cultivating them than he did in being a skilled warrior."

(18) "Yes, by Zeus," said Socrates, "and Cyrus, it seems, had he lived, would have become an excellent ruler; of this there were many proofs provided, but particularly the fact that during the march against his brother, in the fight for the kingdom, it is said that no one deserted Cyrus for the king, while tens of thousands came from the king to Cyrus. (19) I

---

[19] This seems to refer, as the account in IV.18 ff. certainly does, to the younger Cyrus, Xenophon's contemporary and friend and leader of the revolt against his brother, the Persian king Artaxerxes. Yet unlike the elder Cyrus, the founder of the Persian Empire, the younger Cyrus was never in fact "king." (See below, pp. 117–118.)

regard it also as a great proof of virtue in a ruler when others willingly obey him [20] and are willing to remain with him even in terrible dangers. Cyrus' friends fought with him while he lived, and when he was dead they all died fighting near his corpse, except Ariaios; for Ariaios happened to have been ordered to the left wing.[21] (20) It was this Cyrus who is said to have received Lysander [22] with many marks of friendship when he came bringing presents from the allies—as Lysander himself once said in relating the story to a certain host in Megara—and in particular, he said, he displayed to him the pleasure garden in Sardis. (21) After Lysander had wondered at it —that the trees should be so fine, the plantings so regular, the rows of trees so straight, the angles so finely laid, and that so many pleasant scents should accompany them as they walked —wondering at these things, he spoke. 'I, Cyrus, am full of wonder at the beauty [23] of everything,[24] but much more do I admire the one who has measured out and ordered each kind

[20] Or "when others are readily persuaded [*peithōntai*] by him."

[21] Compare *Anabasis* I.8.5 and I.9.31. The commander of all Cyrus' non-Greek troops and his chief lieutenant, Ariaios fled the battle as soon as he learned of Cyrus' death. Later he exchanged oaths of fidelity with the Greeks who had fought under Cyrus, but soon afterward deserted them altogether.

[22] Lysander was a Spartan and commander of the Peloponnesian fleet during the last years of the Peloponnesian War. The occasion and circumstances of his meeting with Cyrus, which took place in 407, are described by Xenophon in the *Hellenica* (I.5.1 ff.); its main object was to secure Persian assistance in the prosecution of the war against Athens. Xenophon does not, however, make mention in the *Hellenica* of the incident related here.

[23] *Kallos*, "beauty," is derived from the adjective *kalos*, which may mean "noble" as well as "beautiful," and which in this translation is usually rendered "fine."

[24] In the Oxford text this phrase is emended to read, in translation: "the beauty of everything here" or "of all these things" (*panta tauta*). The insertion of *tauta* is without manuscript authority.

of thing for you.' (22) On hearing this, Cyrus was pleased and spoke. 'All these things, Lysander, I measured out and ordered myself, and there are some of them,' he said that he said, 'that I even planted myself.' (23) And Lysander said that, looking at him and seeing the beauty of the clothes he wore, perceiving their scent and also the beauty of the necklaces and bracelets and the other ornaments he was wearing, he had spoken and said: 'What do you mean, Cyrus? You planted some of these with your own hands?' (24) And Cyrus had replied, 'Do you wonder at this, Lysander? I swear to you by Mithras: as long as I'm healthy, I never go to dinner until I have worked up a sweat practicing some work of war or farming or at any rate devoting my ambition to some one thing.' (25) And Lysander himself said that on hearing this he took Cyrus' right hand and spoke: 'You, Cyrus, seem to me to be justly happy, for you are happy while being a good man.' "

V

(1) "This, Kritoboulos, I narrate," said Socrates, "because it shows that not even the altogether blessed can abstain from farming. For the pursuit of farming seems to be at the same time some soft pleasure, an increase of the household, and a training of the bodies so that they can do whatever befits a free man. (2) First, the earth bears, to those who work it, what human beings live on, and it bears in addition what they take pleasure in experiencing; (3) then, it provides that with which they adorn altars and statues and are adorned themselves, together with the most pleasant scents and sights; then, it either brings forth or nourishes all manner of sauces [25]—for the art of sheep-breeding is akin to farming—that they may

[25] The Greek word (*opson*) signifies whatever is eaten with bread, i.e., both meat and vegetables.

have something with which, by sacrificing, to win over the gods, as well as something to use themselves. (4) But though providing the good things most abundantly, it doesn't yield them up to softness but accustoms all to bear the cold of winter and the heat of summer. It exercises those who work with their own hands and adds to their strength, and it produces a kind of manliness even in those who are merely concerned with farming, causing them to rise early in the morning and compelling them to move about vigorously. For in the country as in town, the most important actions have always their proper season. (5) Then, if someone wants to defend the city as a horseman, farming is most sufficient for maintaining a horse, or if one is a foot soldier, it provides a vigorous body. The earth also in some degree encourages a love of the toil in the hunt, since it provides the dogs with an easy source of nourishment and at the same time supports wild animals. (6) And not only are the horses and dogs benefited by farming, but they benefit the country in turn, the horse by carrying the caretaker [26] to his concerns early in the morning and allowing him to return late, and the dogs by keeping wild animals from damaging the crops or the sheep and by helping to give safety to solitude. (7) Further, the earth stimulates in some degree the farmers to armed protection of the country by nourishing her crops in the open for the strongest to take. (8) What art makes men more fit for running, throwing, and jumping than does farming? What art brings more gratifications to those who work at it? What affords a more pleasant welcome to the one concerned with it—inviting whoever comes along to take whatever he requires? What welcomes

[26] Evidently, the master. Xenophon uses a poetic and somewhat strange expression (*ho kēdomenos*), literally, "the one who is troubled," "the one who is concerned [for]."

foreigners with more abundance? (9) Where are there more facilities than in the country for passing the winter with an abundance of fire and warm baths? And where can one spend a summer more pleasantly than in the country, amid waters and breezes and shade? (10) What provides more suitable first offerings for the gods or presents ampler feasts? What is more beloved by servants, more pleasant for the wife, more sharply missed by children, or more gratifying to friends? (11) It would seem wonderful to me if any free human being possessed anything more pleasant than this or found a concern at once more pleasant and of greater benefit in life. (12) Furthermore, the earth, being a goddess, teaches justice to those who are able to learn, for she gives the most goods in return to those who serve her best. (13) Then if those engaged in farming and educated to vigor and manliness should at some time be deprived of their works by a multitude of invaders, they would be able—if the god didn't prevent them—being well prepared both in soul and in body, to go into the country of the preventers and take what they needed to maintain themselves. For in war it is often safer to seek to maintain oneself with arms rather than with the instruments of farming. (14) At the same time farming educates in helping others. For in fighting one's enemies, as well as in working the earth, it is necessary to have the assistance of other human beings. (15) The one who is going to farm well, then, must provide himself with eager workers who are willing to obey him; and the one who leads against enemies must devise means to accomplish the same things, by giving presents to those who act as the good ought to act and by punishing those who are disorderly. (16) The farmer must often exhort his workers no less than the general his soldiers; and good hopes are no less necessary to slaves than to the free, but rather more so, that they may be willing to remain. (17) Whoever said that farming is the mother and nurse of all the other arts spoke finely indeed. For when farming goes well, all the other arts also flourish, but when the earth is compelled to lie barren, the other arts almost cease to exist, at sea as well as on the earth."

(18) After having heard this, Kritoboulos said: "In regard to these things, Socrates, you seem to me, at least, to speak finely; but in regard to most of the things of farming,[27] it's impossible for a human being to exercise forethought: sometimes hail, frost, drought, violent rains, blights, and often indeed other things wreck what has been finely conceived and done; sometimes a herd of sheep raised in the finest manner is most miserably destroyed by disease."

(19) After having heard this, Socrates said: "But I supposed you knew, Kritoboulos, that the gods are lords of the works of farming no less than of those of war. Those who are at war you see, I suppose, trying to win over the gods before undertaking warlike actions, and consulting them by means of sacrifices and auguries as to what must or must not be done; (20) but in regard to the actions of farming, do you suppose it any less necessary to propitiate the gods? Know well," he said, "that sensible men attend to the gods out of regard for their crops—the wet and the dry alike—and their oxen and horses and sheep and indeed all their possessions."

VI

(1) "In regard to these things, Socrates," he said, "you seem to me to speak finely, in suggesting that one attempt to begin every work with the gods' favor, since the gods are lords of

[27] Literally, "the things of the farming [art]." The adjective is used, as is common in Greek, with a substantive absent but understood: probably either "knowledge" or "art" is intended.

the works of peace no less than those of war. We shall attempt to do it. But speaking from where you left off in your account of household management, you must attempt to go through what remains of it for us; for having heard what you've said, I now seem to see rather better than before what I must do in order to make a living."

(2) "What then," said Socrates, "if we first recapitulate what we have gone through and agreed upon, that we may attempt in the same way, if we are at all able, to go through the rest so as to agree upon it?"

(3) "It's a pleasant thing, at any rate," said Kritoboulos, "for partners in speeches to go through what they have discussed and agree, as it is for partners in wealth to go over their accounts without dispute."

(4) "Then," said Socrates, "it seemed to us that household management is the name of some kind of knowledge, and the knowledge itself looked to be that by which human beings are enabled to increase households; a household then looked to us to be the totality of possessions, a possession we asserted to be whatever would be beneficial for the life of each, and beneficial things were found to be all things that one knows how to use. (5) Then as it seemed impossible to us to learn all the kinds of knowledge, we joined the cities in repudiating the so-called mechanical arts, because they seem to ruin the bodies utterly and because they enervate the souls. (6) One would have the clearest proof of this, we asserted, if, as enemies were invading the country, one were to seat the farmers and the artisans apart from one another and question each as to whether it seemed better to defend the country or, giving up the earth altogether, to guard the walls. (7) Those who are bound to the earth we supposed would vote to defend it, while the artisans would vote not to fight at all but rather to sit still as they

had been educated to do, neither toiling nor risking danger. (8) We came to the conclusion that for the gentleman the best kind of work and the best kind of knowledge is farming, by which human beings supply themselves with the necessary things. (9) For that kind of work seemed to be at once the easiest to learn and the most pleasant to work at; it seemed to produce at once the finest and most robust bodies, and as for the souls, it seemed least of all to cause any lack of leisure for joining in the concerns of friends and cities. (10) It seemed to us further that farming incites to bravery those who work at it, by bringing forth and nourishing the necessary things outside the fortifications. This manner of living is, as a result, held in highest repute by the cities, for it seems to provide the best and best-willed citizens to the community."

(11) And Kritoboulos: "I seem to be quite sufficiently persuaded, Socrates, that farming is indeed the finest and best and most pleasant way to make a living; but as to what you asserted earlier—that you had learned the causes of some people's farming in such a way as to have everything they need from farming, and in abundance, and of others' working in such a way that farming is not at all lucrative for them—of both these things, it seems to me, I would be pleased to hear you speak, so that we may do what is good and avoid what is harmful."

(12) "What then, Kritoboulos," said Socrates, "if I relate to you from the beginning how I once came together with a man who seemed to me really to be one of those men to whom the name of gentleman is justly applied?"

"I would like very much to hear it," said Kritoboulos, "as I too desire to become worthy of that name."

(13) "I'll tell you, too," said Socrates, "how I came to the consideration of it. A very short time was sufficient for me to go around to the good carpenters, the good smiths, the good

painters, the sculptors, and all the others like them, to see the works of theirs that were reputed to be fine. (14) But as regards those who have the solemn name of gentleman, that I might investigate what sort of work they do to be worthy of being called by it, my soul very much desired to come together with one of them. (15) And first, because the 'fine' is added to the 'good,'[28] whenever I saw a fine-looking man, I would go up to him and try to learn whether I could see the 'good' connected to the 'fine.' (16) But this was not the case, for I seemed to learn that some of those who were fine in outward form were quite depraved in their souls. It seemed best, then, to disregard the fine looks and to go instead to one of those who are called gentlemen. (17) Since I had heard Ischomachos named a gentleman by everyone—by men and women, foreigners and townsmen alike—it seemed best to try to come together with him."

VII

(1) "Seeing him then one day sitting in the colonnade of Zeus the Deliverer, I went over to him, and as he seemed to be at leisure, I sat down with him and spoke. 'Why are you sitting like this, Ischomachos, you who are so unaccustomed to leisure? For I mostly see you either doing something or at least hardly at leisure in the market place.'

(2) " 'Nor would you see me now, Socrates,' said Ischomachos, 'if I hadn't made an appointment to meet some foreigners here.'

" 'When you aren't doing this sort of thing,' I said, 'by the gods, how do you spend your time and what do you do? For I

---

[28] The phrase *kalos kàgathos* [*anēr*], "gentleman," means literally "fine and good [man]." Throughout this passage Socrates plays on the ambiguity of *kalos*, which may mean "external beauty" as well as "nobility."

would like very much to inquire what it is you do in order to be called a gentleman, since you don't spend your time indoors, and the condition of your body hardly looks like that of one who does.'

(3) "And Ischomachos, laughing at my asking what he did to be called a gentleman and rather pleased, or so it seemed to me, spoke. 'I don't know whether some call me by that name when discussing me with you, but surely when they call me to an exchange [29] for the support of a trireme or the training of a chorus, no one,' he said, 'goes looking for "the gentleman," but they summon me clearly,' he said, 'by the name Ischomachos and by my father's name.[30] As to what you asked me, Socrates,' he said, 'I never spend time indoors. Indeed,' he said, 'my wife is quite able by herself to manage the things within the house.'

(4) " 'It would please me very much, Ischomachos,' I said, 'if I might also inquire about this—whether you yourself educated your wife to be the way she ought to be, or whether, when you took her from her mother and father, she already knew how to manage the things that are appropriate to her.' [31]

(5) " 'How, Socrates,' he said, 'could she have known anything when I took her, since she came to me when she was not yet fifteen, and had lived previously under diligent supervision in order that she might see and hear as little as possible and ask the fewest possible questions? (6) Doesn't it seem to you that one should be content if she came knowing only how to take the wool and make clothes, and had seen how the spinning

[29] *Antidosis.* There was an Athenian law according to which a man charged with a public duty could challenge someone he believed richer than himself either to take on the duty or to exchange his property for that of the challenger.

[30] I.e., by his patronymic: "Ischomachos, the son of . . . ."

[31] The expression can also mean "the things that belong to her."

work is distributed among the female attendants? For as to matters of the stomach, Socrates,' he said, 'she came to me very finely educated; and to me, at any rate, that seems to be an education of the greatest importance both for a man and a woman.'

(7) " 'And in other respects, Ischomachos,' I said, 'did you yourself educate your wife to be capable of concerning herself with what's appropriate to her?'

" 'By Zeus,' said Ischomachos, 'not until I had sacrificed and prayed that I might succeed in teaching, and she in learning, what is best for both of us.'

(8) " 'Didn't your wife sacrifice with you and pray for these same things?' I said.

" 'Certainly,' said Ischomachos; 'she promised before the gods that she would become what she ought to be, and made it evident that she would not neglect the things she was being taught.'

(9) " 'By the gods, Ischomachos,' I said, 'relate to me what you first began teaching her. I'd listen to you relating these things with more pleasure than if you were telling me about the finest contest in wrestling or horsemanship.'

(10) "And Ischomachos replied: 'Well, Socrates,' he said, 'when she had gotten accustomed to me and had been domesticated to the extent that we could have discussions, I questioned her somewhat as follows. "Tell me, woman, have you thought yet why it was that I took you and your parents gave you to me? (11) That it was not for want of someone else to spend the night with—this is obvious, I know, to you too. Rather, when I considered for myself, and your parents for you, whom we might take as the best partner for the household and children, I chose you, and your parents, as it appears, from

among the possibilities [32] chose me. (12) Should a god grant us children, we will then consider, with respect to them, how we may best educate them; for this too is a good common to us—to obtain the best allies and the best supporters in old age; (13) but for the present this household is what is common to us. As to myself, everything of mine I declare to be in common, and as for you, everything you've brought you have deposited in common. It's not necessary to calculate which of us has contributed the greater number of things, but it is necessary to know this well, that whichever of us is the better partner will be the one to contribute the things of greater worth." (14) To this, Socrates, my wife replied: "What can I do to help you?" she said. "What is my capacity? But everything depends on you: my work, my mother told me, is to be moderate." (15) "By Zeus, woman," I said, "my father told me the same thing. But it's for moderate people—for man and woman alike—not only to keep their substance in the best condition but also to add as much as possible to it by fine and just means." (16) "Then what do you see," said my wife, "that I might do to help in increasing the household?" "By Zeus," I said, "just try to do in the best manner possible what the gods have brought you forth to be capable of and what the law praises." (17) "And what are these things?" she said. "I suppose they are things of no little worth," I said, "unless, of course, the leading bee in the hive also has charge of works of little worth. (18) For it seems to me, woman," ' he said that he had said, ' "that the gods have used great consideration in joining together the pair called male and female so that it

[32] The expression could also mean either "from among capable men," i.e., men of some wealth and position (cf. XI.10), or "according to their [i.e., the parents'] capabilities."

may be of the greatest benefit to itself in its community. (19) First, that the races of living things may not be extinguished, the pair is brought together for the production of children; then, from this pairing it is given to human beings at least to possess supporters in old age; but then the way of life of human beings is not, as is that of cattle, in the open air, but evidently needs shelter. (20) Still, if human beings are going to have something to bring into the dwellings, someone is needed to work in the open air. For plowing the fallow, sowing, planting, and herding are all works of the open air, and from them the necessary things are gotten. (21) But when these things have been brought into the dwelling, someone is needed to keep them secure and to do the works that need shelter. The rearing of newborn children also needs shelter; shelter is needed for the making of bread from the crop, and similarly for the working of clothes from wool. (22) Since, then, work and diligence are needed both for the indoor and for the outdoor things, it seems to me," ' he had said, ' "that the god directly prepared the woman's nature for indoor works and indoor concerns.[33] (23) For he equipped the man, in body and in soul, with a greater capacity to endure cold and heat, journeys and expeditions, and so has ordered him to the outdoor works; but in bringing forth, for the woman, a body that is less capable in these respects," ' he said that he had said, ' "the god has, it seems to me, ordered her to the indoor works. (24) But knowing that he had implanted [34] in the woman, and ordered her to, the nourishment of newborn chil-

[33] The construction of this sentence in Greek could lead one to believe that something has dropped out of the text at this point. The Oxford editor makes the following conjecture, which, however, lacks manuscript authority: "and that of the man for outdoor ones."

[34] The words for "implant" and "bring forth" have the same root, being related to the word for "nature" (*physis*).

dren, he also gave her a greater affection for the newborn infants than he gave to the man. (25) Since he had also ordered the woman to the guarding of the things brought in, the god, understanding that a fearful soul is not worse at guarding, also gave the woman a greater share of fear than the man. And knowing too that the one who had the outdoor works would need to defend himself should someone act unjustly, to him he gave a greater share of boldness. (26) But because it's necessary for both to give and to take, he endowed both with memory and diligence in like degree, so that you can't distinguish whether the male or the female kind has the greater share of these things. (27) As for self-control in the necessary things, he endowed both with this too in like degree; and the god allowed the one who proved the better, whether the man or the woman, to derive more from this good. (28) Since, then, the nature of each has not been brought forth to be naturally apt for all of the same things, each has need of the other, and their pairing is more beneficial to each, for where one falls short the other is capable. (29) Now," I said, "O woman, as we know what has been ordered to each of us by the god, we must, separately, do what's appropriate to each. (30) The law too praises these things," ' he said that he had said, ' "in pairing man and woman; and as the god made them partners in children, so too does the law appoint them partners.[35] And the law shows that what the god has brought forth each to be capable of is fine as well. It is a finer thing for the woman to stay indoors than to spend time in the open, while it is more disgraceful for the man to stay indoors than to concern himself with outdoor things. (31) But when someone acts in a way

[35] In the Oxford text this phrase is emended to read, in translation: "so too does the law appoint them partners in the household." The insertion of the words for "in the household" is without manuscript authority.

contrary to what the god has brought forth, perhaps in causing some disorder he is noticed by the gods and pays the penalty for neglecting his own works or for doing the woman's
works. (32) And it seems to me," I said, "that the leader of
the bees also toils in this way to accomplish the works that the
god has ordered her to do." "In what way," she said, "are the
works of the leader of the bees similar to the works I must
do?" (33) "In that she remains in the hive," I said, "and
doesn't let the bees be inactive but sends them to the work
whenever some are needed to work outside; she knows what
each of them brings in, receives it, and keeps it secure until it
is needed for use. When the season for using it comes around,
she distributes to each what is just. (34) She also has charge of
the weaving of the cells inside, to see that they are finely and
quickly woven, and when the offspring are born, she is concerned with their nourishment; and once the young are fully
grown and able to work, she sends them out as a colony, with
one of them as leader." (35) "Will it be necessary, then," said
my wife, "for me to do these things as well?" "It will be necessary," I said, "for you to remain indoors and to send out
those of the servants whose work is outside; as for those whose
work is to be done inside, these are to be in your charge;
(36) you must receive what is brought in and distribute what
needs to be expended, and as for what needs to be set aside,
you must use forethought and guard against expending in a
month what was intended to last a year. When wool is
brought to you, it must be your concern that clothes be made
for whoever needs them. And it must be your concern that the
dry grain be fine and fit for eating. (37) There is one thing,
however," I said, "among the concerns appropriate to you,
that will perhaps seem less agreeable: whenever any of the servants become ill, it must be your concern that all be attended."

"By Zeus," said my wife, "that will be most agreeable, at least if those who have been well tended are going to be grateful and feel more good will than before." (38) I admired her reply,' said Ischomachos, 'and spoke: "Isn't it through this kind of forethought that the leader of the hive so disposes the other bees to her that when she leaves the hive, not one of the bees supposes they must let her go, but rather they all follow?" (39) My wife replied: "I wonder whether the works of the leader [36] are not rather yours than mine. For my guarding and distribution of the indoor things would look somewhat ridiculous, I suppose, if it weren't your concern to bring in something from outside." (40) "On the other hand," I said, "it would look ridiculous for me to bring anything in if there weren't someone to keep secure what had been brought in. Don't you see," I said, "how those who are said to draw water with a leaking jar are to be pitied, since they seem to toil in vain?" "By Zeus," said my wife, "they are miserable indeed, if this is what they do." (41) "Other private concerns will prove pleasant for you, woman," I said, "as when you take someone who knows nothing of spinning and make her knowledgeable, so that she is worth twice as much to you; or when you take someone who knows nothing of housekeeping or waiting and make her a knowledgeable, trusted, and skilled waiting maid, worth any sum; or when you're allowed to treat well those who are both moderate and beneficial to your household, and to punish anyone who looks to be wicked. (42) But the most pleasant thing of all: if you look to be better than I and make me your servant, you will have no need to fear that with advancing age you will be honored any less in the household, and

[36] Ischomachos' wife uses the masculine article (*ho*) with *hēgemōn* ("leader") where previously Ischomachos had used only the feminine (*hē*), in the sense "the queen bee."

you may trust that as you grow older, the better a partner you prove to be for me, and for the children the better a guardian of the household, by so much more will you be honored in the household. (43) For the fine and good things increase for human beings, not by ripening like fair fruits,[37] but through the exercise of the virtues in life." I seem to remember saying such things to her, Socrates, at the time of our first discussion." "

VIII

(1) " 'Did you notice, Ischomachos,' I said, 'that she was stirred to diligence by these things?'

" 'Yes, by Zeus,' said Ischomachos. 'I know she once became very upset, and blushed deeply, when she was unable to give me one of the things I had brought in when I asked for it. (2) Seeing she was irritated, I spoke. "Don't be discouraged, woman," I said, "because you can't give me what I happen to ask for. It is indeed clear poverty not to have a thing to use when it's needed; at the same time our present want—to look for something and be unable to find it—is certainly a less painful thing than not to look for it at all, knowing it's not there. But you aren't at fault in this," I said; "rather I am, since I handed over these things to you without giving orders as to where each kind of thing should be put, so that you would know where to put them and where to find them again. (3) There is nothing, woman, so useful or fine for human beings as order. A chorus consists of human beings; when each acts in a chance way, a confusion appears that is unlovely even to look at, but when they act and speak in an ordered manner,

---

[37] "Ripening like fair fruits" translates *ōraiotēs*, a word of rare occurrence and uncertain meaning. It suggests seasonableness, ripeness, and beauty.

the same ones seem worth looking at and worth hearing as well. (4) And, woman," I said, "a disordered army is a thing of the greatest confusion, the easiest prey for its enemies, and for its friends a most inglorious and useless sight—mules, heavy-armed soldiers, baggage carriers, light-armed soldiers, horse-men, and wagons, all together; for how could they march if they were constantly getting in one another's way, the slow marcher obstructing the fast marcher, the fast marcher collid-ing with someone who is standing still, the wagon blocking the horseman, the mule blocking the wagon, the baggage carrier blocking the heavy-armed soldier? (5) And if they had to fight, how could they ever do it in this condition? The ones who were compelled to flee before the attackers would be apt to trample the ones actually under arms. (6) An ordered army, on the other hand, is the finest sight for friends and the most appalling for enemies. What friend wouldn't look with pleasure on a large number of heavy-armed soldiers marching in order, or wonder at the horsemen riding in ordered groups? What enemy wouldn't be terrified by the sight of heavy-armed soldiers, horsemen, targeteers, archers, and slingers, all distinctly arranged and following their rulers in an orderly way? (7) For when they march in order, though there be tens of thousands of them, all march calmly, as one man; the empty spaces are always filled by those coming up from behind. (8) And why else is a trireme laden with human beings a fear-ful thing for enemies and for friends a thing worth looking at, unless it is because it sails quickly? And how else do those who sail in it keep out of one another's way unless it's by sitting in order, bending forward in order, drawing back in order, and embarking and disembarking in order? (9) Disorder is the sort of thing, it seems to me, that would result if a farmer threw together in one place his barley and wheat and peas, and then,

when he needed barley cakes or bread or sauce, had to separate them grain by grain instead of having them already distinctly arranged for use. (10) If you would rather avoid this
confusion, woman, and want to know how to manage our substance accurately, how to find easily whatever is needed for
use, and how to oblige me by giving me whatever I ask for,
then let us choose a place that is appropriate for each kind of
thing and, after putting it there, let us teach the waiting maid
to take the thing from there and to put it back again. In that
way we shall know what's secure and what isn't; for the place
itself will miss the thing that isn't there, a glance will indicate
what needs attention, and the knowledge of where each thing
is will put it quickly into our hands, so that we'll be at no loss
when it comes to using it." (11) And I saw what seemed to
me the finest and most accurate ordering of implements, Socrates, when I went to look over that large Phoenician ship; I saw
there a very great number of implements divided within a
rather small space. (12) Indeed,' he said, 'it takes a great many
implements—wooden things and ropes—to launch and land the
ship, and it sails with much so-called suspended rigging; it is
armed with many devices for use against enemy ships, carries
arms for the men, and brings for the common mess all the implements that human beings use in the house. Besides all this, it
is loaded with the cargo that the owner transports for profit.
(13) And everything I have mentioned,' he said, 'is kept in a
place not much larger than a room proportioned for ten
couches. I noticed that everything is kept in such a way that
nothing obstructs anything else or requires anyone to search
for it, or is so inaccessible or so difficult to remove as to cause
a delay when needed for some sudden use. (14) I found that
the boatswain, the so-called man of the prow, knew so well
the place of each kind of thing that he could say, without
being there, just where everything was kept and how many

there were of each kind, and no less exactly than the knower of letters could say how many letters are in "Socrates" and what their order is. (15) I saw this same one,' said Ischomachos, 'inspecting at his leisure all the things that would have to be used on the ship. And wondering at this examination,' he said, 'I asked him what he was doing. He spoke. "Stranger," he said, "I'm examining how the things in the ship are kept, in case anything should happen," he said, "or in case anything is missing or is awkwardly placed. (16) For when the god raises a storm at sea," he said, "there's no time to search for whatever may be needed or to get out something from an awkward place. The god threatens and punishes the slack. If only he doesn't destroy those who have not gone wrong, one should be satisfied; and if he preserves those who serve him in the finest manner, one should be very grateful," he said, "to the gods." (17) Having observed, then, the accuracy in this arrangement, I said to my wife that we would be very slack indeed if those in ships—which, after all, are rather small—find places for their things and preserve the order among them, even when they are roughly tossed about, and are able even in moments of panic to find what is needed, whereas we, who have large and distinct storerooms in our house for each kind of thing and indeed have a house on solid ground, cannot find a fine place for each of our things where they may readily be found—how could this be anything but the greatest unintelligence on our part? (18) That an ordered arrangement of implements is a good, then, and that it is easy to find in the house an advantageous place for each kind of thing, has been established. (19) But how fine it looks, too, when shoes of any kind are set out in a regular manner; it is fine to see clothes of any kind when they are sorted, as also bedcovers, bronze kettles, the things pertaining to the table, and—what of all things would be most ridiculed, not indeed by the solemn man but by the wit—even pots have a graceful look when distinctly arranged. (20) Indeed, all other things look somehow finer when they are kept in order.[38] Each kind of thing looks like a chorus of implements, and even the space between them looks fine, as everything has been kept out of it—just as a circular chorus is not only itself a fine sight, but even the space within it looks pure and fine. (21) If I am speaking the truth, woman," I said, "it will be possible for us to try these things without suffering much loss or going to much trouble. Nor should we be discouraged, woman," I said, "by the difficulty of finding someone who can learn the places and remember to replace each kind of thing. (22) For we know very well that the whole city has ten thousand times what we have, yet when you tell any one of the servants to buy something for you in the market place, he is never at a loss—every one of them evidently knows where he has to go for each kind of thing. The cause of this," I said, "is nothing other than that everything is kept ordered in its place. (23) But if someone goes looking for another human being—who may at the same time be looking for him—he very frequently gives up before finding him. And the cause of this is nothing other than that there is no ordered place for their meeting." As regards the order of implements and their use, I seem to remember discussing with her things of this sort.' "

IX

(1) " 'What then, Ischomachos?' I said. 'Did your wife seem to listen at all to what you were trying so seriously to teach her?'

---

[38] "Order" here translates the Greek *kosmos*, which often means simply "ornament" (as in IV.23 and IX.6). The usual word for "order," *taxis*, and its derivatives (as in VIII.18 and VIII.22–23), connote by contrast primarily military order.

" 'What else did she do if not promise to be diligent, manifest her very great pleasure, as though she had found some easy
means out of a difficulty, and ask me to order things separately
as quickly as possible in the way I had stated?'

(2) " 'How, then, Ischomachos,' I said, 'did you separately
order them for her?'

" 'What else seemed best to me if not to show her first the
capacity of the house? For it is not adorned with decorations,
Socrates; the rooms were planned and built simply with a view
to their being the most advantageous receptacles for the things
that would be in them, so that each calls for what is suitable to
it. (3) The bedroom, being in an interior part of the house,
invites the most valuable bedcovers and implements; the dry
parts of the dwelling, the grain; the cool places, the wine; and
the well-lighted places, the works and implements that need
light. (4) And I displayed to her the areas for the daily use of
human beings, furnished so as to be cool in summer and warm
in winter. And I displayed to her the house as a whole, and
how it lies open to the south—obviously, so as to be well exposed to the sun in winter and well shaded in summer.
(5) Then I pointed out to her the women's apartments, separated from the men's by a bolted door, so that nothing may be
taken out that shouldn't be and so that the servants may not
produce offspring without our knowledge. For the useful ones,
for the most part, feel even more good will once they have
had children, but when wicked ones are paired together, they
become only more resourceful in their bad behavior. (6) When
we had gone through these things,' he said, 'we then proceeded
to separate our belongings according to tribes. We began first,'
he said, 'by collecting whatever we use for sacrifices. After this
we distinguished the woman's ornaments for festivals, the
man's dress for festivals and war, bedcovers for the women's
apartments, bedcovers for the men's apartments, shoes for

women, shoes for men. (7) Another tribe consisted of arms, another of instruments for spinning, another of instruments for breadmaking, another of instruments for cooking, another of the things for bathing, another of the things for kneading bread, another of the things for the table; and all these things were further divided according to whether they were used every day or only for festivals. (8) We also set apart the expenses for each month from the amount that had been calculated and reserved for the whole year; for in this way we could better see how things would come out at the end. And when we had sorted our belongings according to tribes, we took each kind of thing to its appropriate place. (9) After this, as to the implements the servants use from day to day— those for the making of bread, for cooking, for spinning, and others of this sort—we pointed out to those who would be using them where each must go, handed them over, and gave orders that they be kept secure. (10) Those we use for festivals, for entertaining foreigners, or only from time to time we handed over to the housekeeper, and after pointing out to her their places and counting and making lists of the various kinds of things, we told her to give each what he needed of them, to remember what she had given someone, and when she had got it back, to return it to the place she had taken it from. (11) We chose as housekeeper the one who upon examination seemed to us the most self-controlled as regards food, wine, sleep, and intercourse with men, and who, in addition, seemed to have a good memory and the forethought to avoid punishment for negligence and to consider how, by gratifying us in some way, she might be honored by us in return. (12) We taught her also to feel good will toward us, sharing our delights when we were delighted in some way, and when there was something painful, inviting her aid. We further educated her to be eager to increase the household, making her thoroughly acquainted with it and giving her a share in its prosperity. (13) And we inspired justice in her, honoring the just more than the unjust and displaying to her that they live richer and freer lives than the unjust. We then installed her in the place. (14) But in addition to all these things, Socrates,' he said, 'I told my wife that there would be no benefit in any of this unless she herself was diligent in seeing that the order is preserved in each thing. I taught her that in the cities subject to good laws the citizens do not think it enough merely to have fine laws, but in addition choose guardians of the laws to examine them, to praise the one who acts lawfully, and to punish the one who acts contrary to the laws. (15) Then,' he said, 'I suggested that my wife consider herself a guardian of the laws regarding the things in the house; that she inspect the implements whenever it seems best to her, just as a garrison commander inspects his guards; that she test the fitness of each thing, just as the council tests the fitness of horses and horsemen; and that, like a queen, she praise and honor the deserving, to the limit of her capacity, and rebuke and punish the one who needs such things. (16) In addition,' he said, 'I taught her that she could not be justly annoyed if I gave her many more orders in regard to our possessions than I gave to the servants, displaying to her that the servants share in their master's wealth only to the extent that they carry it, attend to it, or guard it, and that no one of them is allowed to use it unless the lord gives it to him, whereas everything is the master's to use as he wishes. (17) To the one deriving the greatest benefit from its preservation and the greatest harm from its destruction belongs the greatest concern for a thing—this I declared to her.'

(18) "'What then?' I said. 'After your wife had heard these things, Ischomachos, did she at all obey you?'

" 'What else did she do,' he said, 'if not tell me I didn't understand her correctly if I supposed that in teaching her to be concerned with our substance I had ordered her to do something hard. For as she told me,' he said, 'it would have been much harder if I had ordered her to neglect her own things than if she were required to concern herself with the goods of the household. (19) For just as it seems natural,' he said, 'for a sensible woman to be concerned for her offspring rather than to neglect them, so, she said, it's more pleasant for a sensible woman to be concerned for those of the possessions that delight her because they are her own than to neglect them.' "

X

(1) "On hearing that his wife had replied to him in this way," said Socrates, "I spoke. 'By Hera, Ischomachos,' I said, 'you display your wife's manly understanding.'

" 'There are other instances of her high-mindedness that I am willing to relate to you,' said Ischomachos, 'instances of her obeying me quickly in some matter after hearing it only once.'

" 'In what sort of thing?' I said. 'Speak; for to me it is much more pleasant to learn of the virtue of a living woman than to have had Zeuxis display for me the fine likeness of a woman he had painted.'

(2) "Ischomachos then speaks. 'And yet once, Socrates,' he said, 'I saw she had applied a good deal of white lead to her face, that she might seem to be fairer than she was, and some dye, so that she would look more flushed than was the truth, and she also wore high shoes, that she might seem taller than she naturally was. (3) "Tell me, woman," I said, "would you judge me more worthy to be loved as a partner in wealth if I showed you our substance itself, didn't boast of having more substance than is really mine, and didn't hide any part of our

substance, or if instead I tried to deceive you by saying I have more substance than is really mine and by displaying to you counterfeit money, necklaces of gilt wood, and purple robes that lose their color, and asserting they are genuine?" (4) She broke in straightway. "Hush," she said; "don't you become like that; if you did, I could never love you from my soul." "Haven't we also come together, woman," I said, "as partners in one another's bodies?" "Human beings say so, at least," she said. (5) "Would I then seem more worthy to be loved," I said, "as a partner in the body, if I tried to offer you my body after concerning myself that it be healthy and strong, so that I would really be well complexioned, or if instead I smeared myself with vermilion, applied flesh color beneath the eyes, and then displayed myself to you and embraced you, all the while deceiving you and offering you vermilion to see and touch instead of my own skin?" (6) "I wouldn't touch vermilion with as much pleasure as I would you," she said, "or see flesh color with as much pleasure as your own, or see painted eyes with as much pleasure as your healthy ones." (7) "You must believe, woman,"' Ischomachos said that he had said, ' "that I too am not more pleased by the color of white lead or dye than by your color, but just as the gods have made horses most pleasant to horses, oxen to oxen, and sheep to sheep, so human beings suppose the pure body of a human being is most pleasant. (8) Such deceits may in some way deceive outsiders and go undetected, but when those who are always together try to deceive one another they are necessarily found out. For either they are found out when they rise from their beds and before they have prepared themselves, or they are detected by their sweat or exposed by tears, or they are genuinely revealed in bathing."'

(9) "'By the gods,' I said, 'what did she reply to this?'

" 'What else,' he said, 'was her reply, if not that she never did anything of the sort again and tried always to display herself suitably and in a pure state. At the same time she asked me if I could not advise her how she might really come to sight as fine and not merely seem to be. (10) I advised her, Socrates,' he said, 'not always to sit about like a slave but to try, with the gods' help, to stand at the loom like a mistress, to teach others what she knew better than they, and to learn what she did not know as well; and also to examine the breadmaker, to watch over the housekeeper in her distribution of things, and to go about and investigate whether each kind of thing is in the place it should be. In this way, it seemed to me, she could both attend to her concerns and have the opportunity to walk about. (11) And I said it would be good exercise to moisten and knead the bread and to shake out and fold the clothes and bedcovers. I said that if she exercised in this way, she would take more pleasure in eating, would become healthier, and so would come to sight as better complexioned in truth. (12) And a wife's looks, when in contrast to a waiting maid she is purer and more suitably dressed, become attractive, especially when she gratifies her husband willingly instead of serving him under compulsion. (13) On the other hand, women who always sit about in pretentious solemnity lend themselves to comparison with those who use adornments and deceit. And now, Socrates,' he said, 'know well, my wife still arranges her life as I taught her then and as I tell you now.' "

XI

(1) "Then I spoke. 'Ischomachos, I seem to have heard enough for the present concerning the works of your wife, for which indeed you both deserve praise. But as to your own works,' I said, 'tell me now of them, in order that you may

take pleasure in relating the things for which you are highly reputed and that I may be very grateful to you after hearing fully about the works of the gentleman and after understanding them, if I can do so.'

(2) " 'But by Zeus, Socrates,' said Ischomachos, 'it will be a very great pleasure for me to tell you about my constant doings, so that you may also correct me if in anything I do not seem to you to act finely.'

(3) " 'But how could I justly correct a perfect gentleman,' I said, 'especially as I am a man who is reputed to be an idle talker and to measure the air and who is reproached for being poor—which seems to be the most foolish accusation of all? (4) And I would have been greatly discouraged by this charge, Ischomachos, if I had not recently encountered the horse of Nikias, the newcomer, and seen the numerous onlookers who were following it and heard some of them speaking about it; whereupon I approached the groom and asked him if the horse had much wealth. (5) He looked at me as though I had not asked a sane question, and spoke: "How could a horse have wealth?" I was relieved then on hearing that it is permitted a poor horse to become good if it has a soul by nature good. (6) Therefore, as it is permitted me to become a good man, you must fully tell about your works so as to enable me, insofar as I can learn by listening, to imitate you, beginning tomorrow. That is a good day,' I said, 'to begin in virtue.'

(7) " 'You're joking, Socrates,' said Ischomachos, 'but I'll give you an account anyway of the practices with which, as far as I can, I try to occupy my life. (8) Since I seem to have learned that the gods do not permit human beings to prosper unless they understand what they ought to do and are diligent in accomplishing it, and that nevertheless they grant only to some of the prudent and diligent to be happy, and not to oth-

ers, I therefore begin by attending to the gods, and I pray to them and act in such a manner that it may be permitted me to acquire health, strength of body, honor in the city, good will among my friends, and in war noble safety and noble increase of riches.'

(9) "And I, having heard this: 'Is it then a matter of concern with you to be rich, Ischomachos, and having much wealth, to have also the troubles that come from concerning yourself with it?'

" 'What you speak of is certainly a matter of concern with me,' said Ischomachos, 'for it seems to me a pleasant thing, Socrates, to honor the gods magnificently, to aid friends when they need something, and to see that the city is never unadorned through lack of wealth.'

(10) " 'These are fine things you speak of, Ischomachos,' I said, 'and particularly suited to a capable man. Indeed how could it be otherwise? For there are many human beings who cannot live without being in need of others, and many are content if they can provide only what is enough for themselves. But as to those who not only can manage their own households but even produce a surplus which enables them to adorn the city and relieve their friends, how could one hold that they are not men of weight and strength? (11) There are indeed many of us who can praise this sort,' I said, 'but you, Ischomachos, tell me what you began with—how you concern yourself with health and the strength of the body, and how it is permitted you to save yourself nobly in war. As for your money-making,' I said, 'it will be sufficient if we hear of that later.'

(12) " 'But as it seems to me, Socrates,' said Ischomachos, 'these things all follow on one another. For when someone has enough to eat, he stays healthier, it seems to me, if he works it

off in the right manner, and in working it off, he also becomes stronger. If he trains in military matters, he can save himself more nobly, and if he is diligent in the right manner and doesn't grow soft, it is likely he will increase his household.'

(13) " 'I follow you this far, Ischomachos,' I said, 'when you assert that the human being who works off a meal and is diligent and trains himself is more apt to acquire the good things, but as to the kind of toil that is necessary for keeping up one's strength and condition, and as to how one ought to train in military matters, or how one must be diligent in producing a surplus so as to aid friends and strengthen the city—it is with pleasure,' I said, 'that I would hear these things.'

(14) " 'I have accustomed myself, Socrates,' said Ischomachos, 'to rising from my bed at an hour when I can expect to find indoors anyone it happens I need to see. And if there is something I need to do in the city, I use the opportunity to walk there; (15) but if there's no necessity for being in the city, the boy takes my horse into the fields, and I use the occasion for a walk along the road to the fields—which is perhaps a better thing, Socrates, than a walk under a colonnade. (16) When I come to the fields, I examine the work in hand and correct it, if I have something better to suggest, whether it is planting they happen to be doing or plowing the fallow or sowing or gathering in the crops. (17) After this I usually mount my horse and practice a kind of horsemanship as similar as possible to the horsemanship necessary in war, avoiding neither traverses, slopes, ditches, nor streams, though concerned not to lame my horse in the process. (18) When this is done, the boy gives the horse a roll and leads it home, at the same time taking with him into town whatever we need from the country; and I return home, sometimes walking, sometimes at a run, and clean myself up. I then take my morning meal, Soc-

rates, eating just enough to pass the day without being either empty or overfull.'

(19) " 'By Hera, Ischomachos,' I said, 'to me, at any rate, these things are very agreeable. For to make use at the same time of your arrangements regarding health and strength, your training for war, and your concern for riches—all this seems to me quite admirable. (20) And you have given sufficient proofs that you concern yourself with each of these things in the right manner; for we see you generally healthy and strong, with the gods' help, and we know you are spoken of as one of the most skilled in horsemanship and one of the very rich.'

(21) " 'All the same, Socrates,' he said, 'in doing these things I am greatly slandered by many—perhaps you supposed I was about to say I am called a gentleman by many.'

(22) " 'But I was going to ask you about this too, Ischomachos,' I said: 'whether you make it also a concern of yours to be able to give an account of yourself or to require one from another if you should need it.'

" 'Do I not seem to you, Socrates,' he said, 'to practice constantly these very things—to say in my defense that I do not act unjustly toward anyone and treat many well as far as I am able, and to practice accusing human beings by learning that some act unjustly both toward many in private and toward the city and treat no one well?'

(23) " 'But if you are also practiced in interpretation, Ischomachos,' I said, 'clarify this further for me.'

" 'I never cease to practice speaking, Socrates,' he said. 'For either I listen to one of the servants accusing someone or defending himself and I try to cross-examine him, or I blame someone before my friends or praise someone, or I reconcile certain of my intimates by teaching them it is more advantageous to be friends than enemies; (24) or else when we are in the presence of a general, we censure someone, or defend someone who has been unjustly faulted for something, or accuse one another if someone has been unjustly honored. And frequently we deliberate as to what we desire to do, and praise these things, and as to the things we don't want to do, we blame them. (25) Up to now, Socrates,' he said, 'I have many times submitted to a judgment as to what I must suffer or pay.'

" 'Whose judgment, Ischomachos?' I said. 'For this had escaped my notice.'

" 'My wife's,' he said.

" 'And how do you plead your case?' I said.

" 'Very decently, when it's advantageous to tell the truth; but when untruth would be handier, Socrates, by Zeus I am not able to make the worse argument the stronger.'

"And I spoke: 'Perhaps, Ischomachos, you cannot make the untruth true.' "

XII

(1) " 'But don't let me detain you, Ischomachos,' I said, 'if you want to go away.'

" 'By Zeus, Socrates,' he said, 'you're not detaining me. I wouldn't go away in any case until the market was over.'

(2) " 'By Zeus,' I said, 'you're certainly apprehensive about losing your name for being called a gentleman. For now there are perhaps many matters that require your concern, and yet because you made a promise to some foreigners, you are waiting for them, in order not to prove untruthful.'

" 'But those things you speak of, Socrates,' said Ischomachos, 'aren't neglected by me, for I have stewards in the fields.'

(3) " 'When you need a steward, Ischomachos,' I said, 'do

you try to learn where there's a man who is a skilled steward and attempt to buy him, just as when you need a carpenter you learn—I well know—where to look for a skilled carpenter and attempt to get him into your possession, or do you educate the stewards yourself?'

(4) " 'By Zeus, Socrates,' he said, 'I try to educate them myself. For if someone is to be sufficiently diligent when I am away, what must he know other than what I know myself? If I myself am fit to command the works, I may certainly teach another what I know.'

(5) " 'Then mustn't he first feel good will toward you and yours,' I said, 'if he is going to be really sufficient in your place? For without good will what benefit is there in a steward's having any kind of knowledge?'

" 'None, by Zeus,' said Ischomachos, 'but good will toward me and mine is the first thing I try to teach.'

(6) " 'By the gods,' I said, 'how can you teach just anyone you want to feel good will toward you and yours?'

" 'Generosity, by Zeus,' said Ischomachos, 'whenever the gods give us an abundance of some good.'

(7) " 'Are you saying, then,' I said, 'that those who enjoy your goods come to feel good will and want to do something good for you in return?'

" 'I see this as the best instrument, Socrates, for securing good will.'

(8) " 'And if he comes to feel good will toward you, Ischomachos,' I said, 'will he then be a fit steward? Don't you see that while all human beings feel good will toward themselves, so to speak, many of them aren't willing to be very diligent in acquiring the good things that they want?'

(9) " 'But by Zeus,' said Ischomachos, 'when it's stewards of this sort I want to appoint, I teach them to be diligent.'

(10) " 'By the gods,' I said, 'how? For I supposed diligence was something that could in no way be taught.'

" 'Nor is it possible, Socrates,' he said, 'to teach diligence to all without exception.'

(11) " 'For whom, then,' I said, 'is it possible? Try in every way to indicate to me clearly who they are.'

" 'First, Socrates,' he said, 'you couldn't make anyone diligent who lacks self-control in regard to wine; for intoxication inspires forgetfulness of everything that needs to be done.'

(12) " 'Is it only those who lack self-control in this, then,' I said, 'who are incapable of diligence, or others as well?'

" 'No, by Zeus,' said Ischomachos, 'but also those who lack self-control in regard to sleep; for no one could do in his sleep what needs to be done or make others do it.'

(13) " 'What then?' I said. 'Will these be the only ones incapable of being taught this diligence, or are there others in addition?'

" 'It seems to me, at least,' said Ischomachos, 'that those who are mad lovers of Aphrodite cannot be taught to be more diligent about any other thing than they are about this; (14) for it is not easy to find a hope or a concern more pleasant than the concern for one's favorite, nor is there any punishment so harsh as being kept from one's beloved when there is something to be done. So I don't even try to make those diligent whom I understand to be of this sort.'

(15) " 'What then?' I said. 'Are those who are in love with profit also incapable of being educated to diligence in the works of the fields?'

" 'No, by Zeus,' said Ischomachos, 'not at all, but they are very well disposed to such diligence; for nothing else is needed than to point out to them that diligence is profitable.'

(16) " 'And as for others,' I said, 'who are self-controlled in

the things you suggest and who are temperate lovers of profit,[39] how do you teach them to be diligent in the way you want them to be?'

" 'It's very simple, Socrates,' he said. 'When I see they are diligent, I praise them and try to honor them, and when I see they are negligent, I try to do and say things I know will sting them.'

(17) " 'Come, Ischomachos,' I said, 'turn the argument from the diligence of the educated and clarify something about education—whether it's possible for one who is himself negligent to make others diligent.'

(18) " 'No, by Zeus,' said Ischomachos, 'no more than it's possible for someone who is himself unmusical to make others musical. For when the teacher himself sets a bad example in something, it is hard to learn from him to do it in a fine way, and if the master sets an example of negligence, it is hard for the attendant to become diligent. (19) To speak concisely: I seem to have learned that the servants of a bad master are always useless; on the other hand, I have seen the servants of a good master act badly, though not without being punished. But whoever wants to make them diligent must be skilled in surveying and inspecting, be willing to show gratitude to the one who is the cause of things finely done, and not shrink from imposing a proper penalty on the one who is negligent. (20) It seems to me that the barbarian's reply was a fine one,' said Ischomachos, 'when the king of Persia, having chanced upon a good horse and wanting to fatten it as quickly as possi-

---

[39] In XII.15, Socrates, following Ischomachos, speaks of "erotic love" (*erōs*); in XII.16 he replaces the erotic lovers of profit by temperate, "friendly lovers" of profit—not *ēros* but *philia*, the term ordinarily translated "love" in the dialogue. Words related to *erōs* occur elsewhere only in VI.12, where the verb *eran* is translated "desire."

ble, asked one of those who seemed to be clever in regard to horses what most quickly fattens a horse, and he is said to have answered, "the master's eye." And so in other things, Socrates,' he said, 'it is under the master's eye that fine and good works are done.' "

XIII

(1) " 'When you have impressed upon someone, and with particular firmness, that he must be diligent in the way you want,' I said, 'is he then fit to become a steward, or is there some other thing to be learned in addition if he is to be a fit steward?'

(2) " 'Yes, by Zeus,' said Ischomachos, 'it still remains for him to understand what is to be done and when it is to be done and how; for if he does not, how is a steward any more beneficial than a doctor who is diligent in visiting his patient day and night and yet doesn't know what would be advantageous for him?'

(3) " 'And if he learns the work that is to be done,' I said, 'will he need anything in addition, or will this be your perfect steward?'

" 'I suppose he must learn at least to rule the workers,' he said.

(4) " 'Then do you,' I said, 'educate the stewards to be fit to rule?'

" 'I try, at least,' said Ischomachos.

" 'But how, by the gods,' I said, 'do you educate them in this matter of ruling human beings?'

" 'In a very ordinary way, Socrates,' he said, 'so that you will perhaps laugh on hearing it.'

(5) " 'This is not a laughing matter, Ischomachos,' I said. 'For whoever is able to make rulers of human beings can evi-

dently teach them also to be masters of human beings, and whoever can make them masters can also make them kings. And so the one who can do this seems to me to be worthy of great praise rather than laughter.'

(6) " 'Other living things, Socrates,' he said, 'learn to obey in these two ways: by being punished when they try to disobey, and by being well treated when they serve eagerly. (7) Colts learn to obey the colt breakers by getting something that's pleasant to them when they obey and getting into trouble when they disobey, until they become subservient to the mind of the colt breaker; (8) and puppies, though they are far inferior to human beings both in mind and tongue, nevertheless learn in the same way to run in a circle and do somersaults and many other things. For when they obey, they get something that they need, and when they are negligent, they are punished. (9) As for human beings, it's possible to make them more obedient by speech as well, by displaying to them how advantageous it is for them to obey; and yet for slaves the education that seems fit only for beasts is effective also in teaching them to obey, for in gratifying their bellies to the extent they desire, you can accomplish much with them. But the ambitious natures among them are spurred by praise as well. For some natures are as hungry for praise as others are for food and drink. (10) These things, then, which I do in the expectation of having more obedient human beings for my use, I teach to those I want to appoint as stewards, and I second them also in the following ways: I make sure that the clothing and the shoes I must supply to the workers are not all alike, but rather some are worse and some better, so that I may be able to honor the stronger one with the better things and give the worse things to the worse. (11) For it seems to me, Socrates,' he said, 'that it is a great discouragement to the good

when they see that the work is done by themselves and yet that they receive the same as those who aren't willing to toil or risk danger when there is need of it. (12) I myself, therefore, in no way consider that the better and the worse deserve to receive equal things, and when I see that the stewards have given the best things to those who are worth the most, I praise them, but if I see someone being honored before others through flattery or some other favor that benefits no one, I do not neglect the matter, Socrates; rather I reprimand the steward and try to teach him that what he is doing is not to his own advantage.' "

XIV

(1) " 'But when he has become fit to rule, Ischomachos,' I said, 'so as to make the others obedient, do you then consider him the perfect steward, or does the one who has everything you've spoken of still need something in addition?'

(2) " 'Yes, by Zeus,' said Ischomachos, 'he must abstain from the master's things and not steal anything. For if the one who manages the crops should dare to make off with them, and the works ceased to be lucrative, what benefit would there be in entrusting him with the farming concerns?'

(3) " 'Do you then undertake to teach justice as well?' I said.

" 'Certainly,' said Ischomachos, 'but I find it's a teaching not all readily obey. (4) Nevertheless, taking some things from the laws of Drakon and some from those of Solon, I try,' he said, 'to lead the servants to justice. For it seems to me,' he said, 'that those men laid down many of their laws with a view to the teaching of this sort of justice. (5) For it is written there that thefts are to be punished, and that if someone is taken in the act of stealing, he is to be imprisoned, or if he resists, put to death. It's evident,' he said, 'that in writing these things, they wanted to make sure that base profit would not be lucrative for the unjust. (6) Adopting some things, then, from these laws,' he said, 'and others from the laws of the king of Persia, I try to make the servants just in respect to what they have under their management. (7) For the first kind of law only punishes those who go wrong, but the laws of the king not only punish those who act unjustly, but they also benefit the just; so that when they see the just becoming rich, many of those who are unjust and lovers of profit are very careful to refrain from acting unjustly. (8) But if I perceive some,' he said, 'who try to act unjustly though they have been well treated, I make it clear that I have no use for anyone so incorrigibly greedy. (9) On the other hand, if I learn of some who are induced to be just, not only through having more than others as a result of their justice, but also through desiring my praise, I treat them as free men, not only enriching them but honoring them as gentlemen. (10) For it seems to me it is in this, Socrates,' he said, 'that the ambitious man [40] differs from the man who loves profit—in his willingness to toil when there is need of it, to risk danger, and to abstain from base profits, for the sake of praise and honor.' "

XV

(1) " 'But when you have inspired in someone a desire that the good things be yours, and you have inspired in the same one a diligence in securing them for you, when in addition you have seen to it that he possesses knowledge as to how each kind of work is to be done so as to provide greater benefits, when in addition you have made him fit to rule, and when fi-

[40] Literally, "the man who loves honor."

nally he is as pleased as you would be at exhibiting a rich harvest, I will no longer ask whether someone of this sort still needs something in addition; for it seems to me a steward of this sort would already be worth very much. But Ischomachos,' I said, 'don't omit this one thing, which we passed over very lazily in the argument.'

(2) " 'What?' said Ischomachos.

" 'You were saying,' I said, 'that it is most important to learn how each kind of work must be performed; there would be no benefit in diligence, you asserted, if one didn't know what must be done and how it must be done.'

(3) "Then Ischomachos spoke. 'Are you suggesting I teach you the art of farming itself, Socrates?'

" 'It is perhaps this art that makes those rich who know it,' I said, 'while those who don't know it live a poor life no matter how much they toil.'

(4) " 'Now, Socrates,' he said, 'hear of the philanthropy of this art. For as it is most beneficial and pleasant to work at, the finest and most beloved of gods and human beings, and in addition the easiest to learn, how can it be anything but well-bred? For, indeed, of living things we call those well-bred that are fine, great, beneficial, and at the same time gentle toward human beings.'

(5) " 'I seem to have learned sufficiently what you were saying, Ischomachos,' I said, 'as regards what the steward must be taught; I seem to have learned in what way you asserted you made him feel good will toward you, and in what way a fit ruler and just. (6) But when you said that the one who is going to concern himself with farming in the right manner must learn what is to be done and how and when, for each kind of thing—these things, it seems to me,' I said, 'we have passed over somewhat lazily in the argument. (7) It

is as if you should say that the one who is going to be able to write down what is dictated to him and read what is written must know letters. Had I heard this, I would have heard indeed that one must know letters, but I suppose I wouldn't know letters any better for knowing this. (8) In the same way, I am by now readily persuaded that the one who is going to concern himself with farming must know it, but I don't know how to farm any better for knowing this. (9) But if it should seem best to me right now to take up farming, I would seem to be like the doctor who visits his patients and examines them and yet doesn't know what would be advantageous for them. So that I may not be of this sort, then,' I said, 'teach me the works of farming.'

(10) " 'But really, Socrates,' he said, 'farming is not as difficult to learn as the other arts, where the one who is being taught must wear himself out in the learning before the work he does is worth what it takes to feed him; but partly by seeing others at work and partly by listening, you would know straightway, and well enough to teach someone else, if you wanted to. And I think you know very much about it,' he said, 'without being aware of it. (11) For the other artisans in some way conceal the most important features of their arts; among farmers, on the other hand, the one who plants in the finest manner would be very pleased if someone watched him do it, and similarly with the one who sows in the finest manner; and if you asked him about something that was finely done, he would not conceal from you how he did it. (12) And so it appears, Socrates,' he said, 'that farming also renders those who are engaged in it extremely well-bred in their characters.'

(13) " 'That is a fine preface,' I said, 'and not such as to turn your listener from questioning. As it is easy to learn, then, you must on that account describe it to me more fully. It is

not a disgrace for you to teach something that is easy, and rather more disgraceful by far for me not to know it, especially if it happens to be useful.' "

XVI

(1) " 'First of all, Socrates,' he said, 'I want to display this to you: that part of farming is not at all hard which is called most complicated by those who describe farming most accurately in speech and who do the least work themselves. (2) For they assert that one who is going to farm in the right manner must first know the nature of the earth.'

" 'And they are right to say it,' I said. 'For the one not knowing what the earth has the power to bear would not, I suppose, know what he ought to sow or plant.'

(3) " 'It's possible to understand what it can and cannot bear,' said Ischomachos, 'simply by looking at the crops and trees on a neighbor's land. And once someone understands this, there is no advantage in fighting against the god. For he wouldn't obtain more of the necessary things by sowing and planting what he himself needs rather than what the earth is pleased to bring forth and nourish. (4) But if the earth cannot display its capacity on account of the inactivity of the owners, it is often possible to understand more of the truth about it from a neighboring place than from inquiring of a neighboring human being. (5) And even lying waste it displays its nature, for if it brings forth fine wild products, it can, if tended, bear fine domesticated ones. Thus even those who are not very experienced in farming can understand the nature of the earth.'

(6) " 'But it seems to me, Ischomachos,' I said, 'that I am sufficiently reassured as to this: that I mustn't abstain from farming out of fear that I don't understand the nature of the

earth. (7) Indeed, I remember the practice of fishermen,' I said, 'whose work is at sea, who don't stop to look and don't even slacken their course as they sail by the fields, and yet who, when they see the crops in the earth, do not hesitate to declare which kind of earth is good and which bad, and to blame the one and praise the other. And, in fact, for the most part I see them declaring the same kind of earth to be good as do those who are very experienced in farming.'

(8) " 'At what point, then, Socrates,' he said, 'do you want me to begin reminding you of farming? For I know I'll tell you many things concerning how to farm that you already know.'

(9) " 'It seems to me, Ischomachos,' I said, 'that I would be pleased to learn first—what particularly becomes a man who is a philosopher—how I might work the land, if I wanted to, so as to get the greatest amount of barley and wheat.'

(10) " 'Do you know, then, that it's necessary to prepare the fallow for sowing?'

" 'I do know it,' I said.

(11) " 'What if we began to plough the earth in winter?' he said.

" 'It would be mud,' I said.

" 'Does the summer seem better to you?'

" 'The earth will be too hard for the team,' I said.

(12) " 'Probably the work ought to be begun in the spring,' he said.

" 'It's likely,' I said, 'that the earth will be easier to spread if it is plowed at that time.'

" 'And it is then, Socrates,' he said, 'that the undergrowth, being turned up, provides manure for the earth, while it has not yet shed its seeds so as to bring forth more. (13) For I suppose you understand this too, that if the fallow is going to be good, it must be purified of weeds and baked as much as possible by the sun.'

" 'Certainly,' I said, 'and I believe it must necessarily be this way.'

(14) " 'Do you hold, then,' he said, 'that these things can come about in any other way than by turning over the earth as often as possible during the summer?'

" 'I know with some accuracy,' I said, 'that there is no other way to keep the weeds from taking root or to dry them out with the heat, or to have the earth baked by the sun, than to work the team in the middle of the summer and in the middle of the day.'

(15) " 'Or if human beings should make the fallow by digging up the ground,' he said, 'isn't it quite evident that they also must separate the earth and the weeds?'

" 'And scatter the weeds over the surface,' I said, 'that they may dry out, and turn the earth, that the raw part of it may be baked.' "

XVII

(1) " 'As regards the fallow, Socrates,' he said, 'you see how the same things seem best to both of us.'

" 'They seem best indeed,' I said.

" 'But as regards the season for sowing, Socrates,' he said, 'do you know any other way than to sow in that season which all the human beings before us who have tried it, and all those who try it now, understand to be best? (2) For when the autumnal time comes, all human beings look to the god to find out when he will send rain to the earth and allow them to sow.'

" 'Indeed, Ischomachos,' I said, 'all human beings understand this, and also that they shouldn't willingly sow in dry ground

—because, evidently, those who sow before the god bids them to have to wrestle with many punishments.'

(3) " 'Then all human beings,' said Ischomachos, 'are of like mind in these matters.'

" 'As regards what the god teaches,' I said, 'it happens that all think alike, as for example in winter it seems better to all to wear heavy clothing, if they are able, and it seems better to all to light a fire, if they have wood.'

(4) " 'But in this matter of sowing,' said Ischomachos, 'many differ, Socrates, as to whether the early sowing is best, or the middle, or the latest.'

" 'And the god,' I said, 'does not manage the year in an orderly way; rather one year is finest for the early sowing, another for the middle, another for the latest.'

(5) " 'Do you believe it's better, then, Socrates,' he said, 'for someone to choose one of these sowings, whether he has much or little seed to sow, or rather to begin with the earliest sowing and continue right through the latest?'

"And I spoke. (6) 'To me, Ischomachos, it seems best to share it among all the sowings. For I believe it is much better always to have enough grain than to have very much at one time and not enough at another.'

" 'In this at any rate, Socrates,' he said, 'you, the learner, are of like mind with me, the teacher, even when you are the first to declare your mind.'

(7) " 'What of this?' I said. 'Is there a complicated art to casting the seed?'

" 'By all means, Socrates,' he said, 'let's examine this too. That the seed must be cast from the hand you know, I take it,' he said.

" 'I have seen it,' I said.

" 'But there are some who can cast it evenly,' he said, 'and others who cannot.'

" 'In this, then,' I said, 'the hand needs practice, like the hand of a lyre player, so that it will be able to serve the mind.'

(8) " 'Certainly,' he said. 'But what if the earth is in some places lighter and in others heavier?'

" 'What do you mean?' I said. 'That the lighter is the weaker, and the heavier the stronger?'

" 'I mean that,' he said, 'and I ask you this question: whether you would give equal seed to each kind of earth, or if not, to which kind you would give more.'

(9) " 'I hold to adding more water to the stronger wine,' I said, 'and to imposing the greater burden on the stronger human being if something needs to be carried; and if certain persons needed maintenance, I would order the more capable to maintain more of them. But as to whether weak earth becomes stronger,' I said, 'when someone puts a greater crop in it —as would be the case with oxen—this you must teach me.'

(10) "Ischomachos spoke, laughing. 'But you're joking, Socrates,' he said. 'Know well, however,' he said, 'after you've put the seed in the earth, and after the first shoots appear from the seed during that time when the earth takes much nourishment from heaven, if you plow them in again, they become food for the earth, which then has an access of strength, as if from manure; but if you allow the earth to go on nourishing the seed until you have the crop, it is hard for the weak earth to bring much of a crop to maturity. It is hard also for a weak sow to nourish many excellent pigs.'

(11) " 'Do you mean, Ischomachos,' I said, 'that less seed must be put into the weaker earth?'

" 'Yes, by Zeus,' he said, 'and you agree, Socrates, when you say you hold that all weaker things should be ordered to do less.'

(12) " 'For what purpose, Ischomachos,' I said, 'do you send out hoers to work on the grain?'

" 'You surely know,' he said, 'that there is much rain in winter.'

" 'How could I not know it?'

" 'Let us suppose, then, that some of the grain is covered with mud as a result of the rain, and that some of it is exposed at its roots by the flow of water. And often weeds spring up with the grain as a result of the rain and choke it.'

" 'It's likely,' I said, 'that all these things happen.'

(13) " 'Does it seem to you, then,' he said, 'that the grain needs some assistance under these circumstances?'

" 'Very much so,' I said.

" 'What does it seem to you they could do to assist the muddied grain?'

" 'They could remove the earth,' I said.

" 'And what of the grain that has been exposed at its roots?' he said.

" 'They could replace the earth around it,' I said.

(14) " 'What if the weeds springing up with the grain should choke it,' he said, 'and rob it of its nourishment, just as useless drones rob the bees of the nourishment they have worked to get and to store up?'

" 'One should cut out the weeds, by Zeus,' I said, 'just as one should expel the drones from the hive.'

(15) " 'Does it seem plausible to you, then,' he said, 'that we should send out hoers?'

" 'Certainly. But I am reflecting, Ischomachos,' I said, 'on the effect of introducing good likenesses. For you aroused me much more against the weeds by speaking of drones than you did by speaking of the weeds themselves.' "

XVIII

(1) " 'But after this,' I said, 'the likely thing is reaping. Teach me what you know about this too.'

" 'Unless, at any rate,' he said, 'it looks as if you know the same things about it as I do. You know that the grain must be cut.'

" 'How could I not know it?' I said.

" 'When you cut it, then,' he said, 'do you stand with your back to the wind or facing it?'

" 'Not facing it,' I said; 'for I suppose it is hard on the eyes and the hands to reap with the husk and the sharp ears blowing in one's face.'

(2) " 'And would you cut the ears at the top,' he said, 'or close to the earth?'

" 'If the stalk of grain was short, I, at least,' I said, 'would cut lower down, that the chaff might be more fit for use; if it was tall, I hold I would do right to cut it in the middle, that the threshers might not be troubled with added toil or the winnowers with something they do not need. As for what is left in the earth, I believe it would benefit the earth if it were burned, or if thrown in with the manure, would swell the manure supply.'

(3) " 'You see, Socrates,' he said, 'you are caught in the act: you know the same things about reaping that I do.'

" 'Probably I do,' I said, 'and I want to consider whether I know also about threshing.'

" 'Certainly you know,' he said, 'that they thresh the grain with beasts of burden.'

(4) " 'How could I not know?' I said. 'And I know that oxen, mules, and horses are alike called beasts of burden.'

" 'And you believe they know only how to tread the grain when they are driven?' he said.

" 'What else would beasts of burden know?' I said.

(5) " 'But that they will cut just what is required, and that the threshing will be even—to whom does this belong, Socrates?

" 'Evidently,' I said, 'to the threshers. For by turning over what is untrodden and throwing it under their feet, it is evident they would keep the threshing floor even and quickly finish the work.'

" 'You are not at all behind me,' he said, 'in understanding these things.'

(6) " 'And after this, Ischomachos,' I said, 'we will purify the grain by winnowing it.'

" 'Tell me, Socrates,' said Ischomachos, 'do you know that if you begin to the windward side of the threshing floor, the chaff will be carried over the whole floor?'

" 'That is a necessity,' I said.

(7) " 'It's likely, then,' he said, 'that it will fall on the grain.'

" 'It would be quite something,' I said, 'if the chaff were carried across the grain to the empty part of the threshing floor.'

" 'But what if one began winnowing,' he said, 'from the lee side?'

" 'It is evident,' I said, 'that the chaff would end at once in the chaff receiver.'

(8) " 'But when you have purified the grain,' he said, 'as far as the middle of the floor, will you winnow the remaining chaff while the grain is still spread out, or after you have heaped the purified portion in a narrow space in the center?'

" 'After I have heaped up the purified grain, by Zeus,' I said, 'so that the chaff may be carried to the empty part of the threshing floor and I may not have to winnow the same chaff twice.'

(9) " 'You, Socrates,' he said, 'might even be able to teach another how the grain may be most quickly purified.'

" 'I knew these things,' I said, 'without being aware of it. And for some time I have been thinking whether I might know how to pour gold, play the flute, and paint, without being aware of it. For no one taught me these things any more than farming; but I have seen human beings practicing the other arts, just as I have seen them farming.'

(10) " 'Haven't I been telling you for some time,' said Ischomachos, 'that farming is the most well-bred art, because it's the easiest to learn?'

" 'Come, Ischomachos,' I said, 'I know that; for I know the things pertaining to sowing, though without having been aware that I knew them.' "

XIX

(1) " 'Is the planting of trees,' I said, 'part of the art of farming?'

" 'It is,' said Ischomachos.

" 'How is it, then,' I said, 'that I knew the things pertaining to sowing but don't know the things pertaining to planting?'

(2) " 'Don't you know them?' said Ischomachos.

" 'How could I?' I said. 'I know neither in what kind of earth one should plant nor to what depth one should dig for the plant nor how wide or tall the plant should be when put in nor how the plant should be placed in the earth in order to grow best.'

(3) " 'Come, then,' said Ischomachos, 'learn what you don't know. I know you've seen the kinds of trenches they dig for plants,' he said.

" 'Many times,' I said.

" 'Have you ever seen one of them deeper than three feet?'

" 'Never, by Zeus,' I said, 'deeper than two and a half.'

" 'What of this: have you ever seen one more than three feet in width?'

" 'Never, by Zeus,' I said, 'more than two.'

(4) " 'Come, then,' he said, 'answer me this: have you ever seen one less than a foot in depth?'

" 'Never, by Zeus,' I said, 'less than one and a half. For the plants would be uprooted in digging about them,' I said, 'if they were planted too near the surface.'

(5) " 'You know this sufficiently, then, Socrates,' he said, 'that they do not dig deeper than two and a half feet or less than one and a half.'

" 'I must necessarily have seen this,' I said, 'since it's so obvious.'

(6) " 'What of this?' he said. 'Do you recognize drier and wetter earth when you see it?'

" 'The earth around Lykabettos and that similar to it,' I said, 'seems to me to be dry, and the earth in the Phalerian marsh and that similar to it, to be wet.'

(7) " 'Would you then dig a deep pit for the tree in the dry earth,' he said, 'or in the wet?'

" 'In the dry, by Zeus,' I said; 'for if you dug a deep one in the wet earth, you would find water, and you wouldn't be able to plant in water.'

" 'You seem to me to speak finely,' he said. 'But once the pits are dug—have you ever seen when each kind of plant ought to be put in them?'

(8) " 'Certainly,' I said.

" 'Then as you want them to grow as quickly as possible, do you suppose that if you put prepared earth under it, the vine cutting would take root faster through this soft earth than through unworked earth in hard ground?'

" 'It's evident,' I said, 'that it would sprout more quickly through prepared than through unworked earth.'

(9) " 'Earth would then have to be put under the plant.'

" 'How could it not be?' I said.

" 'But do you believe that the cutting would rather take root if you placed it upright, looking toward heaven, or if you placed it on its side in the prepared earth, like an overturned gamma?'

(10) " 'That way, by Zeus,' I said, 'for there would be more eyes beneath the earth; it is from the eyes that I see the plants sprouting up above. And I believe the eyes beneath the earth do the same thing. With many shoots growing in the earth, the plant would, I believe, sprout quickly and vigorously.'

(11) " 'As regards these matters,' he said, 'you happen to understand the same things I do. But would you only pile the earth around the plant,' he said, 'or would you pack it down firmly?'

" 'I would pack it down, by Zeus,' I said, 'for if it weren't packed down, I know well that the rain would turn the unpacked earth to mud, and the sun would dry it up completely; so there would be a danger that during the rains the plants would rot from dampness, or that there would be too much heat at the roots and they would wither from dryness or from the porousness of the earth.' [41]

(12) " 'As regards the planting of vines also, Socrates,' he said, 'you happen to understand all the same things I do.'

" 'Should one plant the fig in the same way?' I said.

" 'I suppose so,' said Ischomachos, 'and all the other fruit trees. But which of the fine procedures in the planting of the vine would you reject in the other plantings?'

(13) " 'How shall we plant the olive, Ischomachos?' I said.

" 'You are testing me in this too,' he said, 'which you know best of all. For you surely see that a deeper pit is dug for the

[41] The Greek phrases for "during the rains" and "or from the porousness of the earth" are bracketed in the Oxford text, though apparently with no manuscript authority.

olive, as it is dug mostly along the roadsides; you see that stems belong to all the young plants; you see,' he said, 'that mud covers the heads of all the roots, and that the upper part of every plant is protected.'

(14) " 'I see all these things,' I said.

" 'Since you see them, then,' he said, 'what is it you don't understand? Are you ignorant, Socrates,' he said, 'of how to place shells over the mud?'

" 'By Zeus,' I said, 'there is nothing you say that I am ignorant of, Ischomachos, but I am thinking again why it was, when you asked me some time ago whether in general I knew how to plant, that I denied it. For I seemed to have nothing to say regarding how one should plant; but since you have undertaken to question me on each thing by itself, I answer the very things that you—who are said to be a clever farmer—assert you understand yourself. (15) Is it the case, then, Ischomachos,' I said, 'that questioning is teaching? For I come to learn,' I said, 'just by the way you question me about each kind of thing; for by leading me through what I know, you display to me that what I held I didn't know is similar to it and persuade me, I suppose, that I know that too.'

(16) " 'If, then, in regard to a piece of money,' said Ischomachos, 'I questioned you as to whether it was fine or not, would I be able to persuade you that you knew how to distinguish the fine from the counterfeit piece? Or if I questioned you about flute players, would I be able to persuade you that you knew how to play the flute—or about painters, or about others of this sort?'

" 'Perhaps,' I said, 'for you persuaded me that I am a knower of farming, though I know no one ever taught me this art.'

(17) " 'It's not the same, Socrates,' he said; 'but some time ago I told you that farming is such a philanthropic and gentle

art that it makes those who see and hear of it at once knowers of it. (18) For it teaches many things itself,' he said, 'about how one may use it in the finest manner. The vine running up trees, whenever it has a tree nearby, straightway teaches that it must be supported; by spreading its leaves while its bunches are still tender, it teaches that shade must be provided for whatever is at that season exposed to the sun; (19) by shedding the leaves when it's time for the grapes to be sweetened by the sun, it teaches that it must be stripped and the fruit brought to ripeness; and by showing, in its productiveness, some bunches mature and others still unripe, it teaches that each must be gathered as it swells to maturity, in the same way that figs are gathered.' "

XX

(1) "Then I spoke. 'If the things pertaining to farming are so easy to learn, Ischomachos, and all know equally well what ought to be done, how is it that all do not do equally well, but rather some live in abundance and have a surplus, while others cannot provide even the necessary things but run into debt besides?'

(2) " 'I'll tell you, Socrates,' said Ischomachos. 'It isn't the knowledge or the ignorance of the farmers that causes some to be well off and others to be poor; (3) you would never hear any argument,' he said, 'to the effect that the household is ruined because the sower didn't sow evenly, or because he didn't plant in straight rows, or because being ignorant of what kind of earth bears vines, someone planted them in infertile soil, or because someone was ignorant of the good that comes from preparing the fallow for sowing, or because someone was ignorant of how good it is to mix manure with earth; (4) but it is more usual to hear this: "The man doesn't get any grain from

his fields because he isn't diligent in sowing them or in providing manure"; or "The man has no wine because he isn't diligent in planting the vines or in getting the ones he has to bear fruit"; or "The man has neither olives nor figs because he isn't diligent and does nothing to get them." (5) Such things, Socrates, are the cause of the differences between farmers and their faring so differently, rather than the fact that some seem to have invented something wise for use in the work. (6) So it happens that some generals are better and others worse in certain works of strategy, though they don't differ from one another in mind but rather clearly in diligence. For what all the generals understand—and most private men—only some of the rulers act on, while some do not. (7) For example, all understand that in war it's better for the marchers to march in an orderly manner if they are to fight well when there is need of it. But though they understand this, some act on it, and some don't. (8) All know it's better to post guards day and night before the camp. But some are diligent in doing this, and some are not diligent. (9) And when they pass through narrow places, isn't it very difficult to find someone who does not understand that it's better to occupy commanding positions beforehand than not to? But here again some are diligent in doing it, and some are not. (10) And all say that manure is excellent in farming, and they see that it's readily available; yet though they know with some accuracy how it becomes available and how easily a lot can be gotten, some are diligent in seeing that it is collected, and some neglect it entirely. (11) Again, the god provides rain from above, the hollow places are filled with water, and the earth provides weeds of every kind, of which the earth must be purified by the one who is going to sow; but if someone should throw the weeds he has removed into the water, time itself would produce those things in which the earth takes pleasure. For what kind of weed, what kind of earth, does not become manure in stagnant water? (12) And what sort of attention the earth needs— whether it is too damp for sowing or too salty for planting— everyone understands, as well as how water may be drained by ditches and how a salty soil may be corrected by mixing with it any number of unsalty materials whether moist or dry; but as regards these things, some are diligent, and some are not. (13) Even if someone were in every way ignorant of what the earth can bear, and had never had an opportunity to see its crops and plants or to hear the truth about it from anyone, isn't it still much easier for any human being to test the earth than to test a horse, and much easier indeed than to test another human being? For it doesn't show itself deceptively, but reveals simply and truthfully what it can do and what it cannot. (14) It seems to me that the earth excellently distinguishes those who are bad and inactive by providing what is easily learned and understood. For it's not possible with farming, as it is with the other arts, for the ones who don't work at it to make the excuse that they don't know it, since all know that the earth does well when it is well treated; (15) but inactivity as regards the earth is a clear accusation of a bad soul. For no one persuades himself that a human being would be able to live without the necessary things; but he who neither knows no other money-making art nor is willing to farm obviously intends to live from stealing or robbing or begging, or is altogether irrational.' (16) He said that it makes a great difference as to whether farming is lucrative or not when someone with a number of workmen is diligent in seeing to it that his workers remain at work the entire time, and another isn't diligent in this respect. 'For it makes a difference when one man of ten works the entire time, as it makes a difference when another man leaves before the time is up. (17) Indeed, to let human beings take it easy in their work during a whole day easily makes a difference of half the whole amount of work. (18) Just as in traveling it sometimes happens that two human beings, though both are young and healthy, differ from each other in speed by as much as a hundred stadia in two hundred when one does what he set out to do and keeps walking, while the other, idle and easy in his soul, lingers at fountains and shady places, looks at the sights, and hunts soft breezes. (19) In the same way, as regards work, there is a great difference in what is accomplished by those who do what they have been ordered to do, and those who don't do it but find excuses for not working and are allowed to take it easy. (20) To perform one's work in a fine way, or to lack in diligence, makes as much difference as to be wholly at work or wholly inactive. When those who are digging to purify the vines of weeds dig in such a manner that the weeds come up in greater numbers and finer than before, how could you deny that this is inactivity? (21) These, then, are the things that wreck households, much more than any great deficiencies in knowledge. For when constant expenditures flow from the households while the work isn't lucrative with respect to the expenditures, one ought not to wonder if there is want instead of a surplus. (22) For those who are capable of diligence, however, and who farm with utmost vigor, my father taught me, and himself practiced, a most effective way of making money from farming. He never allowed me to buy land that had been worked previously, but whatever through neglect or the incapacity of its possessors lay inactive and unplanted—this he encouraged me to buy. (23) For he used to say that cultivated land costs a great deal of money and permits of no improvement; he held that what permits of no improvement does not provide the pleasures of that which does, and supposed that every possession or creature on its way to becoming better affords a greater delight. But nothing shows greater improvement than inactive land when it becomes fertile. (24) Know well, Socrates,' he said, 'we have by now made many pieces of land worth many times their old value. And this invention, Socrates,' he said, 'while worth very much, is very easy to learn; now that you have heard of it, you know it as well as I do, and you may go away and teach it to another, if you want to. (25) Indeed, my father neither learned it from anyone nor meditated very deeply to find it out; he used to say that he desired land of that sort because of his love of farming and his love of toil, in order to have something to do and at the same time to feel pleasure while being benefited. (26) It seems to me, Socrates,' he said, 'my father was by nature the Athenian most in love with farming.'

"And I, on hearing this, asked him: 'Did your father then keep in his possession the land he had worked, Ischomachos, or did he sell it if he could get a lot of money for it?'

" 'He sold it, by Zeus,' said Ischomachos; 'but he bought other land at once, inactive land, because of his love of work.'

(27) " 'You are saying, Ischomachos,' I said, 'that by nature your father was really no less a lover of farming than the merchants are lovers of grain. For the merchants, from an excessive love of grain, sail the Aegean, the Euxine, and the seas of Sicily in search of the place they hear has the greatest quantity of it; (28) and when they have gotten as much as they can, they bring it across the sea, stowing it in the ship they sail in themselves. And when they need money, they don't dispose of it at random wherever they happen to be, but rather wherever they hear that grain is particularly valued [42] and highly regarded by human beings, there they take it and to them they

[42] The word for "value" (*timē*), here as in XX.24, means literally "honor."

offer it. In a similar way, somehow, your father appears to have been a lover of farming.'

(29) "Ischomachos spoke in response to this. 'You're joking, Socrates,' he said; 'but I still hold that those who sell the houses they have built and then build others are no less lovers of housebuilding.'

" 'By Zeus, Ischomachos,' I said, 'I swear to you, I trust what you say: all believe by nature that they love those things by which they believe they are benefited.' " [43]

XXI

(1) " 'But I am thinking, Ischomachos,' I said, 'how well you have shaped your whole argument to aid your contention; for you contended that the art of farming is the easiest of all to learn, and I am now in every way persuaded, by all you've said, that this is indeed the case.'

(2) " 'By Zeus,' said Ischomachos, 'but, Socrates, as regards what is common to all actions—to farming, politics, household management, and war—I mean ruling, I agree with you that some men differ very much from others in mind; (3) in a trireme, for example,' he said, 'which needs a full day's rowing to cross the open sea, some of the boatswains are able to say and do such things as whet the souls of human beings and cause them to toil willingly, while others are so lacking in mind that they accomplish the voyage in more than twice the time. In the one case the boatswain and those who obey him leave the ship dripping sweat and full of praise for one another, while the others arrive without having worked up a sweat, hating

[43] In the Oxford text the first *nomizein* ("believe") is bracketed, with some slight manuscript authority. Its deletion would make the translation of the whole sentence read: "by nature they love those things by which they believe they are benefited."

their supervisor and being hated by him. (4) And generals differ from one another in the same way,' he said, 'for some provide soldiers who aren't willing to toil or risk danger, who don't consider it worth their while to obey and don't do so except by necessity, but rather take pride in opposing the ruler; these generals provide soldiers who don't know enough to be ashamed if some disgraceful thing happens to them. (5) But the divine, good, and knowing rulers, when they take over soldiers of this sort and often others worse than they, make of them soldiers who are ashamed to do anything disgraceful, who suppose it is better to obey, who are indeed, one and all, proud to obey, and who toil undiscouraged when toil is needed. (6) Just as a love of toil may arise in certain private men, so in a whole army under good rulers there may arise both a love of toil and an ambition to be seen doing some fine act by the ruler himself. (7) Rulers toward whom their followers are disposed in this way are the ones who become the strongest rulers, not, by Zeus, those who excel the soldiers in bodily condition, who excel in javelin-throwing or archery, who have the best horses, and who risk danger in the forefront of the cavalry or of the targeteers, but rather those who are capable of inspiring the soldiers to follow them through fire and through every danger. (8) One might justly call these great-minded, and many who follow them understand it; indeed, he may plausibly be said to march with a strong arm whose mind so many arms are willing to serve, and he is really a great man who can do great things by means of the mind rather than by means of strength. (9) In the same way in private work, whether the one in charge is a steward or a supervisor, those who can make the workers eager, energetic, and persevering in the work are the ones who accomplish the most good and produce a large surplus. (10) But, Socrates,' he said, 'if the master

—who can harm the bad workers and honor the eager ones to the greatest degree—himself appeared at the work and the workers did nothing remarkable, I would not admire him, but if on seeing him they were stirred and every one of the workers was filled with spirit and a love of victory and an ambition to outdo the others, then I would assert he had something of a kingly character. (11) And this is the greatest thing, it seems to me, in any work where something is achieved by human beings, in farming as in any other. Yet I do not say, by Zeus, that it's possible to learn by seeing it or by hearing of it once, but I assert that the one who is going to be capable of it needs education, a good nature, and most of all, to become divine. (12) For it seems to me that this good—to rule over willing subjects—is not altogether a human thing but, rather, divine; it is clearly given only to those who have been genuinely initiated into the mysteries of moderation; but tyrannical rule over unwilling subjects, it seems to me, they give to those whom they believe worthy of living like Tantalus in Hades, who is said to spend unending time in fear of a second death.' "

▨▨▨▨▨ Xenophon's Socratic Discourse

by LEO STRAUSS

ꝋꝋꝋꝋꝋ Introduction

The Great Tradition of political philosophy was originated by Socrates. Socrates is said to have disregarded the whole of nature altogether in order to devote himself entirely to the study of ethical things. His reason seems to have been that while man is not necessarily in need of knowledge of the nature of all things, he must of necessity be concerned with how he should live individually and collectively.[1]

For our precise knowledge of Socrates' thought we depend on Plato's dialogues, Xenophon's Socratic writings, Aristophanes' *Clouds*, and some remarks of Aristotle. Of these four men Xenophon is the only one who, while knowing Socrates himself, showed by deed that he was willing to be a historian. Hence it would appear that the primary source for our knowledge of Socrates should be the Socratic writings of Xenophon.

This appearance is rendered powerless by a powerful prejudice which emerged in the course of the nineteenth century and is today firmly established. According to that prejudice Xenophon is so simple-minded and narrow-minded or philistine that he cannot have grasped the core or depth of Socrates' thought.

Against this prejudice we appeal in the first place to the judgment of Winckelmann, who praised "the noble simplicity and quiet grandeur" of the writings of "the unadorned great Xenophon" and who found grace, i.e., that which reasonably pleases, in Xenophon as distinguished from Thucydides and

[1] Aristotle, *Metaphysics* 987b1–2; Xenophon, *Memorabilia* I.1.12–16; Plato, *Apology of Socrates* 19b1–d7, 38a1–6.

therefore compared Xenophon to Raphael while comparing Thucydides to Michelangelo.[2] We appeal in the second place to the silent judgment of Machiavelli. Our age boasts of being more open to everything human than any earlier age; it is surely blind to the greatness of Xenophon. Without intending it, one might make some discoveries about our age by reading and rereading Xenophon.

We cannot study here all writings of Xenophon; we cannot even study here his four Socratic writings. To make a judicious choice, we must consider the purport of his Socratic writings. The largest of them is the *Apomnēmoneumata*, or as it is ordinarily called in Latin, the *Memorabilia*, which we may provisionally translate *Reminiscences* or *Memoirs*. Its purport would be more obvious than it is if it were entitled, as it has sometimes been quoted by both ancient and modern writers, *Memorabilia Socratis*. Its genuine title does not so much as hint at its peculiar subject. We remember what we have seen or heard, and Xenophon had seen many things and especially many deeds and heard many speeches of men other than Socrates. In particular he himself had accomplished some deeds and pronounced some speeches which he considered worth remembering, since he devoted to them the bulk of his *Kyrou Anabasis* (*Cyrus' Ascent*). In fact the title *Memoirs* would seem to fit his *Cyrus' Ascent* much better than the work that he entitled *Memoirs*. Certainly *Cyrus' Ascent* is as inadequate a title for the work so named as *Memoirs* is as a title for the work devoted exclusively to Socrates: the account of Cyrus' ascent is completed at the end of the first book of the work, while the remaining six books deal with the descent of the Greeks led by Xenophon. Certain it is that Xenophon did not

[2] J. J. Winckelmann, *Ausgewählte Schriften und Briefe*, ed. Walter Rehm (Wiesbaden: Dieterich, 1948), pp. 22, 37, 46, 119.

regard what he remembered of his own deeds and speeches as his recollections par excellence: his most memorable experience was the deeds and speeches of Socrates. After all, we remember not only what we have heard or seen but also what we have learned;[3] and Xenophon's teacher par excellence, or the man whom he admired more than any other man, was Socrates.[4]

Xenophon does not state the subject or intention of the *Memorabilia* at the beginning of that work. He opens it rather abruptly by saying that he had often wondered about Socrates' condemnation by the Athenians. He then quotes the indictment and refutes it at length (I.1-2). Thereafter he declares his intention "to write down as much as [he] can remember" of how Socrates "seemed to [him] to benefit those who were together with him." This broad statement indicates the subject matter of all the rest, i.e, of the bulk of the work (I.3 to the end).[5] The *Memorabilia* consists then of two main parts of very unequal length: the refutation of the indictment and Xenophon's recollections concerning Socrates' benefiting his companions. The habit of benefiting people is identified by Xenophon with justice, as he makes clear in the peroration of the *Memorabilia*. The bulk of the *Memorabilia* is then meant to set forth or to praise Socrates' justice. As for the first part, it is meant to refute the indictment, i.e., the assertion that Socrates had committed certain unjust acts; by refuting the indictment, Xenophon shows therefore that Socrates was just in the narrow sense of the term, i.e., that he did not commit crimes or act against the law. Thus the *Memorabilia* as a whole is devoted to proving Socrates' justice.

[3] *Mem.* I.4.13, II.7.7, IV.3.11; *Apol. Socr.* 6.
[4] Cf. *Mem.*, end.
[5] Cf. also, e.g., I.4.1; II, beginning; III, beginning; and IV, beginning.

We shall then tentatively assume that the three other Socratic writings are not devoted to Socrates' justice. It is hardly necessary to say that this does not mean that they are devoted to Socrates' injustice. It means that they are devoted to Socrates *tout court* or to Socrates even if he transcends justice. It is obvious that the consideration of Socrates' justice does not exhaust the praise or the truthful presentation of Socrates. In the very peroration of the *Memorabilia*, Xenophon makes a distinction between Socrates' justice and his prudence (*phronesis*), among other things. Shortly before, he mentions the fact that Socrates' knowledge extended to subjects the knowledge of which is not beneficial.[6] Even granting that justice is a kind of wisdom or knowledge, wisdom or knowledge is surely more comprehensive than justice. This would mean that Xenophon has set a definite limit to his treatment of Socrates in the *Memorabilia* and that he goes beyond that limit in his other Socratic writings.

Xenophon divides all activities of men, and hence in particular those of Socrates, into what they say, what they do, and what they think or silently deliberate.[7] This distinction seems to underlie the distinction among his three Socratic writings other than the *Memorabilia*, as would appear from their openings. This would mean that the *Oeconomicus* is devoted to Socrates' speaking or conversing, the *Symposion* to Socrates' (and other gentlemen's) (playful) deeds, and the *Apology of Socrates* to Socrates' deliberating (on a certain subject). Accordingly, the *Oeconomicus* would be Xenophon's Socratic *logos* or discourse par excellence.

[6] IV.7.3–5.
[7] *Mem.* I.1.19; cf. IV.3, beginning; and *Anabasis* V. 6.28.

▣▣▣▣▣ The title and the opening

The title *Oeconomicus* reminds one of three other Xenophontic titles: *Hipparchikos*, *Kynegetikos*, and *Tyrannikos*. *Tyrannikos* is the alternative title of the *Hieron*, a dialogue, although not a Socratic dialogue; the *Hipparchikos* and the *Kynegetikos* are treatises in which Xenophon speaks throughout in his own name. Each of these three works teaches an art: the art of the cavalry commander, the art of hunting, and the art of the tyrant. The *Oeconomicus* teaches the art of the manager of the household (*oikonomos*). The manager of the household may be good at his work or bad at it; but the *oikonomikos*, i.e., the man who possesses the art of managing the household, is by this very fact a good manager of the household.[1]

According to Xenophon's Socrates, the art of managing the household is one of the highest arts, if not the highest. It differs from the political or royal art only or almost only in regard to the size of the area which it manages.[2] It surely is not inferior to the art of generalship. Socrates could have taught the art of generalship as well as the art of managing the household but, as is shown by the *Oeconomicus*, he taught only the peaceful art of managing the household (or of farming) as distinguished from the warlike art.[3]

We must here make a somewhat polemical remark without which we today cannot understand the *Oeconomicus*. Xeno-

[1] Cf. *Mem.* III.4.7, III.4.11, III.4.12.
[2] *Mem.* III.4.12 and IV.2.11.
[3] Cf. *Oec.* I.17 and VI.1.

phon was a military man, a great practitioner and teacher of
the military art. He also was a great admirer of Socrates. From
the premises that the military art is admirable and that Socrates
was admirable he did not, however, draw the wrong conclusion that Socrates was admirable because he was outstanding as a soldier.[4] On the contrary, the soldier whom he
seems to have admired most—Cyrus, the founder of the
Persian Empire—and Socrates stand at opposite poles of the
universe of his writings. It cannot be emphasized too strongly
that all we know of Socrates as a soldier from the primary
sources we know through Plato and in no way through Xenophon (or through Aristophanes). This is all the more remarkable since Xenophon had a strong reason for speaking of the
military excellence or prowess of Socrates. In a defense of Socrates it certainly would not have been out of place at least to
hint at Socrates' citizen-virtue as shown in war; Xenophon fails
to do so. In a number of chapters of the *Memorabilia* we see
Socrates engaged in conversations with military men about
military matters; in one of these chapters Socrates' interlocutor
mentions the Battle of Delion, in which, as Plato tells us in the
Apology of Socrates, the *Laches*, and the *Symposion*, Socrates
participated and even distinguished himself; neither Xenophon,
nor Socrates, nor Socrates' interlocutor so much as alludes to
the mere presence of Socrates at that battle.[5] It is true that
Xenophon's Socrates appears to be well informed on military
matters; but it is impossible to assert on the basis of Xeno-

---

[4] "It is important to notice the way Plato insists on the military reputation of Socrates. It accounts for the interest taken in him by *Meno*,
Xenophon and others at a later date" (John Burnet, *Greek Philosophy*,
I [London: Macmillan, 1928], 137, n. 2). (The italics are not in the
original.)

[5] *Mem.* III.5.4.

phon's writings that Socrates owed his military knowledge in any way to his military experience; on the contrary, we find him who at that time must have been a mature, if not oldish, man inquiring from another Athenian citizen about the best way to come safely through war and to train oneself in war-like things.[6] In Xenophon's enumerations of Socrates' virtues, manliness, the virtue of war, is not mentioned.[7] Xenophon speaks only once of Socrates' noble conduct as a soldier; he says that Socrates showed his justice (not his manliness) "both in civil life and in campaigns"; but while he adduces four instances of his justice as shown in civil life, he does not adduce a single instance of his justice as shown in war.[8] Socrates was a man of peace rather than of war. It should go without saying that a man of peace is not the same as a pacifist.

What we said when speaking about the title should suffice as a provisional answer to the question why *the* Socratic discourse of Xenophon is devoted to Socrates' teaching the art of managing the household.

The *Oeconomicus* opens as follows: "I once heard him discourse [converse] on the management of the household as well, in about these words. 'Tell me, Kritoboulos,' he said." The *Oeconomicus* opens then abruptly, almost as abruptly as the *Hellenica*, which opens with the expression "Thereafter." The *Hellenica* thus appears to be simply a continuation of another book and, at least at first glance, a continuation of Thucydides' *War of the Peloponnesians and the Athenians;* the abrupt beginning of the *Hellenica* conceals the profound difference between Thucydides' history and Xenophon's history. Similarly,

[6] *Oec.* XI.3, XI.11, XI.13.
[7] *Mem.*, end; *Apol. Socr.* 14, 16.
[8] *Mem.* IV.4.1–4.

the abrupt beginning of the *Oeconomicus* creates the impression that that work is simply a continuation of the *Memorabilia* and thus conceals the profound difference between the *Memorabilia*, the work devoted to Socrates' justice, and Xenophon's Socratic discourse *tout court*. The opening of the *Oeconomicus* reminds one above all of the opening of *Memorabilia* II.4, i.e., of the chapter which opens the section on friendship.[9] That section consists of two parts, the first being devoted to Socrates' general speeches about friendship and the second to how Socrates helped his friends when they were in need. The interlocutor in the most extensive speech of the first part is the same Kritoboulos who is the interlocutor in the *Oeconomicus*. One of the interlocutors in the second part is Kriton, Kritoboulos' father. Kriton and his sons were farmers. Kriton was eager to mind his own business,[10] i.e., he was an economist rather than a politician. The conversation recorded or presented in the *Oeconomicus* takes place in the presence of Xenophon, one of the friends of Socrates and of Kritoboulos.[11] Xenophon was likewise present when Socrates attempted to warn Kritoboulos against the dangers of love, and in particular of kissing beautiful youths. On that occasion, however, Socrates' interlocutor was Xenophon himself. That conversation with Xenophon is the only Socratic conversation with Xenophon that is recorded in Xenophon's Socratic writings. It is distinguished by another peculiarity: Xenophon is the only interlocutor of the Socratic Xenophon who is ever called by his urbane master "you wretch" and "you fool." That is to say, the only Xenophontic character ever treated by the Xeno-

[9] *Mem.* II.4–10. Cf. also II.5, beginning.
[10] *Mem.* II.6, II.9; I.2.47–48. Cf. Plato, *Euthydemus* 291, bottom–292, top.
[11] I.1, III.12.

phontic Socrates in a manner reminiscent of Strepsiades' treatment by the Aristophanean Socrates is Xenophon.[12]

We must keep in mind the question whether there is a connection between the themes "management of the household" and "friendship."

[12] *Mem.* I.3.8–13; cf. *Clouds* 378, 492–493, 628–629, 646, 655, 687.

𒀸𒀸𒀸𒀸𒀸 A definition of household management (Chapter I)

Socrates opens the conversation by asking Kritoboulos without any preparation whether "management of the household" is the name of a science, of a branch of knowledge, "as medicine, smithing, and carpentry are." Socrates begins almost as abruptly as Xenophon. Hence we do not know why he chooses the particular question that he chooses. If that question should be the most appropriate question to address to Kritoboulos, we would be driven to wonder why Xenophon chose Kritoboulos as the interlocutor of Socrates in *the* Socratic discourse. We know still less why Socrates chooses the three examples of branches of knowledge, with smithing in the center. On Kritoboulos' answering in the affirmative, Socrates asks him whether, just as we would be in a position to say of the three branches of knowledge which he now calls arts what the work of each is, we might be able to say what the work of management of the household is. Kritoboulos replies that it seems to be the job of a good manager of the household to administer his household well. Kritoboulos' answer is not simple or straightforward: he qualifies it by "it seems" (or "it is thought to be"), and he defines only what one kind of manager of the household, namely the good one, does. Perhaps he is influenced by Socrates' calling management of the household a science or art: not everyone possesses an art and still less this or that art, and yet everyone—everyone worth speaking about—possesses a household and hence manages it; the art of managing a household, however, is peculiar to those who manage their households well. One could therefore find that Kritoboulos' definition of the good manager of the household is tautological. That this is not the case appears from Socrates' next question: could the good manager of the household not also manage well the household of another man, provided he himself is willing to do so and the other man entrusts to him his household—just as a carpenter can do a carpenter's job for others as well as for himself? On Kritoboulos' replying in the affirmative, Socrates infers that the man who possesses the art of managing households could, even if he were quite poor (i.e., if he had no household of his own), earn pay by managing another man's household, just as a house builder who possesses no house of his own earns pay by building other men's houses and uses part of his pay for living in a rented house.[1] Kritoboulos grants to Socrates that there is no necessary relation between the art of managing the household and one's own household, or in other words that the art of managing the household is as transferable to what is not one's own as the political art.[2] He adds the remark that a man would earn ample pay if he managed another man's household so well as to increase it. According to Kritoboulos, managing the household is then in the best case increasing it. He prepared this disclosure by speaking in his reply to Socrates' earlier question, not of managing the household, but of managing it well. While the divorce of management of the household from "one's own" was due to Socrates, the understanding of management of the household in terms of increase is due to Kritoboulos.[3] Socrates is for the

[1] Cf. *Symp.* 4.4.
[2] Leo Strauss, *What Is Political Philosophy?* (Glencoe, Ill.: Free Press, 1959), p. 82.
[3] Cf. I.4, I.6, I.16, II.2.

time being silent on the change made by Kritoboulos, but this does not prevent him from adopting it later on.

It is now necessary to make clear what a household is. Socrates asks Kritoboulos, "What does a household seem to us to be?" Kritoboulos had hitherto spoken twice of what seemed to him, and once of what seemed (what was generally thought) to be the case; he had stated his opinion or a generally held opinion. Socrates had hitherto only addressed questions to him, so that what seemed to Socrates, Socrates' opinion, did not come to sight. Now he asks Kritoboulos what "our" opinion, i.e., the opinion, among others, of Socrates is. Whatever Kritoboulos will reply, we shall not hear Socrates' opinion but Kritoboulos' opinion of Socrates' opinion. The opinion stated by Kritoboulos will prove to be untenable; this does not prevent Socrates from calling it "our opinion" (I.7): Socrates is not overly concerned with underlining the difference between the interlocutor's initial opinion and his own opinion. Socrates, we may say, has no wish to humiliate Kritoboulos. In agreement with this, both Socrates and Kritoboulos underline the fact that the corrected opinion is Kritoboulos', and not Socrates', opinion; they do this by emphasizing "I" and "thou" respectively when speaking of the corrected opinion. This is not to deny that Socrates' responsibility for the corrected opinion is brought out shortly thereafter with all the clarity one could desire.[4] According to Kritoboulos' initial opinion, a man's household is the whole of his possessions, regardless of whether they are his house, in his house or out of his house, in the city in which he lives or elsewhere. Yet since, as Socrates points out, men frequently possess enemies, it follows that a man's enemies are part of his household. When confronted with this consequence, Kritoboulos immediately admits that it would be ridiculous if a man

[4] Cf. I.7, I.9, I.12, I.15, with XII–XIII.

were to receive pay for increasing the owner's enemies. We note in passing how much Kritoboulos is interested in the possibility that Socrates had opened up for him that the household be managed for pay by a propertyless man on behalf of the owner of the household. According to the drift of the reasoning, the household has now proved to be the whole, not of a man's possessions, but of his good or useful possessions. Or, as Kritoboulos suggests, harmful things, including harmful possessions, are not things of use, or wealth (*chrēmata*), or money at all. This however means that the household must be understood altogether without any regard to "possessions" and with exclusive regard to "usefulness."

In trying to make clear the corrected opinion which he still insists on imputing to Kritoboulos, Socrates uses first the example of a man who buys a horse and, not knowing how to use it, suffers harm; that horse would not belong to his wealth. We may then say that a man's household consists not simply of all things useful to him but of all things which he knows how to use; knowledge seems to be the sole title to property. One cannot avoid this consequence by saying that a thing useless to a man becomes useful to him by his selling it, i.e., not by knowledge; for in order to make the thing in question useful to him, he must know how to sell it and how to use the money which he gets for it. The useless thing will surely not become part of wealth by the mere fact that it is sold, or given, to someone who also does not know how to use it. A ruinous mistress is as little part of a man's household as henbane. Socrates does not raise here the question regarding the status of an economical mistress like Aspasia (cf. III.14), but he elicits from Kritoboulos the reply that for a man who knows how to use his friends for his benefit, the friends are money, by Zeus! The same is true of enemies, for, while enemies desire to harm one, they may well be used for one's own benefit if one possesses the necessary ability. This is confirmed by the fact pointed out by Socrates that many households of private men and of tyrants have been increased through war and perhaps even through usurpation of political power at home.

It remains then true that a man's household consists of all things which are useful to him or which he knows how to use; one does not have to add that the things in question must also be his justly or legally, e.g., through purchase. To say the least, Socrates and Kritoboulos are silent here on justice or legality.[5] To know how to use a thing means to know how to use it well, and ultimately how to use it well with a view to one's life (cf. VI.4). Fully stated, the thought suggested by Socrates and imputed by him to Kritoboulos is to the effect that all good things belong to the wise men, and only to them.[6] As we have seen, this thought is arrived at if one starts from the premise that only what is good or useful to a man belongs to him. That premise was explicitly acted upon by Xenophon's Cyrus when he was still a boy attending a school of justice in Persia. A big boy possessing a small coat had taken away a big coat that belonged to a small boy and had given him his own coat. Cyrus judged that through this action both boys were better off, for each had now what fitted him. For this judgment Cyrus was beaten by his teacher of justice, who said that the question was not what was fitting but what was just or legal.[7] It seems that according to Xenophon the just or legal is not simply the same as the good. To this extent he, or his Socrates, transcended justice or looked at things from the

---

[5] Contrast Chapter I with VII.15, e.g.

[6] Cicero, *Republic* I.27; *De finibus* III.75.

[7] *Cyropaedia* I.3.16–17.

point of view of the good as distinguished from that of justice. This does not mean of course that he simply rejected justice or legality. We see this at once if we consider the extreme
view regarding mine and thine at which one arrives by thinking through Socrates' argument with Kritoboulos, namely, the
view according to which all good things belong to the wise
man, and only to him. For according to Socrates, the wise man
needs very little for himself,[8] and if he is thought to make use
of his property, i.e., of all things, by distributing it properly
according to the needs or merits of his fellow men, his life
would be most troublesome or miserable and hence not a wise
man's life. It is then wiser to return to Kritoboulos' implicit
beginning or to the common-sense view and to take it for
granted that a man's household consists in the first place of
what is his by law, regardless of whether it is useful to him or
not.

At this point of the argument Kritoboulos raises his first
objection: there are men who possess both property and the
required kinds of knowledge and yet do not wish to work and
thus fail to increase their households; the wish to work seems
to be as necessary for successful management of the household
as knowledge. Socrates rejects this addition: the men of whom
Kritoboulos speaks are slaves. Socrates seems to mean that a
free man does not require an incentive different from his
knowledge, or that virtue is knowledge and nothing but
knowledge, or that knowledge overcomes everything obstructing it. Kritoboulos contradicts Socrates again: the men whom
he has in mind are not only free men, but some of them are
even held to be the offspring of noble sires, and they possess
either warlike or peaceful branches of knowledge, which,

[8] *Mem.* I.6.10–11.

however, they are unwilling to employ. We see again that arts of war can be as conducive to increasing one's wealth as peaceful arts. In his refutation of Kritoboulos' objection Socrates assumes that the men of whom Kritoboulos speaks pray or wish to be happy, i.e., rich; Kritoboulos tacitly grants this assumption. Socrates also assumes that one cannot be or remain rich without taking the trouble required for that end; a man who wishes to be rich and does not to wish to work toward that end is irrational; his thought is obscured by beings whose slave he is or who rule him. Kritoboulos does not know who those invisible rulers are. Swearing for the first time, and in fact for the only time in the first chapter—Kritoboulos had already sworn five times—Socrates denies that they are invisible; they are quite manifest, namely, the vices like softness of the soul; another class of the rulers in question consists of certain deceptive Ladies who pretend to be pleasures but eventually reveal themselves as pains. Kritoboulos is still not satisfied. His third objection is to the effect that he knows of men who work hard and inventively and nevertheless fail miserably as managers of their households. Socrates rejoins that these men are slaves of harsh masters, some of greed, some of lechery, some of other things of this kind. This rejoinder is strange, for Kritoboulos had implicitly excluded human beings enslaved by vices of the sort now mentioned by Socrates; Socrates seems too eager to maintain by hook or by crook that possession of a household, knowledge of how to increase it, and willingness to work hard and shrewdly to this effect are the complete conditions for the increase of one's household. That they are not is brought out by Socrates much later, in his reply to Kritoboulos' fourth and last objection—a reply which immediately precedes the final recapitulation of the conversation with Kri-

toboulos.[9] In the meantime Socrates had shown to Kritoboulos that the best manner of managing one's household is
farming. Kritoboulos is satisfied with this suggestion but draws
Socrates' attention to unforeseeable things like droughts and
diseases of cattle which sometimes ruin the work of the
farmer. Socrates is not surprised: success in farming depends
on the gods no less than success in war; hence the farmer must
serve the gods, in particular by sacrificing to them. Socrates
had already spoken spontaneously on the economic significance of sacrifices in the second chapter. His silence, in the
first chapter, on piety as an indispensable ingredient of the
management of the household may provisionally be explained
as a consequence of the abstraction there practiced by him
from justice or legality, for piety depends on law.[10] Be this as
it may, Socrates concludes the reasoning of the first chapter by
contrasting the ruinous effect of enslavement by the harsh
masters or mistresses in question with the sometimes beneficent
effect of enslavement by enemies who are gentlemen.

[9] V.18–20. Cf. also the wording of the beginning of Kritoboulos' speech
in V.18 with the wording of the beginning of his speech stating his first
objection in I.16.
[10] *Mem.* IV.3.16, IV.6.2–4.

The turn to the examination of Kritoboulos and Socrates (Chapter II)

"Biographers of eminent persons are prone to ignore or slur over these harshly practical considerations." "The Muse of History must not be fastidious." [1]

If a man teaches an art in a treatise, he does not necessarily become of interest to his readers. The case is different if an art is taught conversationally, as in the *Oeconomicus*. In reading the first chapter we could not help making some observations about the difference between the contribution of Socrates and that of Kritoboulos. The difference between Socrates and Kritoboulos becomes the theme in the second chapter. That difference is not external to the subject matter (the management of the household) but goes to its root.

The turn from the art to its practitioners is begun by Kritoboulos. Without being bidden by Socrates to do so, he examines himself and finds that he will not be prevented by the vices or bad desires just mentioned or alluded to from increasing his household; but he knows that he does not know how to increase his household; he therefore asks Socrates for guidance —unless Socrates believes that "we" (Kritoboulos and his family) are already sufficiently wealthy and therefore not in need of increasing "our" wealth. Kritoboulos has then an inkling that he ought to learn how to increase his wealth, but he obviously has not done anything toward the acquisition of that

[1] Winston Churchill, *Great Contemporaries* (New York: Putnam, 1937), pp. 204, 263.

knowledge. Socrates' conversation with him about the management of the household has reminded him of his neglected duty: Socrates began that conversation in order to remind him of his neglect of his duties. We are free to suspect that Socrates did this at the request of his contemporary Kriton, whose influence on his son Kritoboulos might have been altogether insufficient, perhaps because he admired Socrates more, much more than his own father. Accordingly, the *Oeconomicus* would also belong to the Socratic conversations that show how Socrates helped his friends when they were in need. We would thus begin to understand the silent reference at the very beginning of the *Oeconomicus* to the very beginning of the section on friendship in the *Memorabilia*.

Kritoboulos had asked Socrates whether he thinks that "we" are sufficiently wealthy already. This gives Socrates an occasion to misunderstand him or to pretend to misunderstand him, as if Kritoboulos might also wonder whether Socrates too was already sufficiently wealthy and hence not in need of increasing his wealth. Socrates states without hesitation that he is sufficiently wealthy already, whereas Kritoboulos is, in Socrates' view, quite poor. Kritoboulos must laugh at Socrates' reply, for, as Socrates himself states, Kritoboulos is more than a hundred times as wealthy as Socrates. Yet, as Socrates explains, measured by Kritoboulos' needs, or more precisely by the pomp which he has assumed and by what people think of him, his wealth, even if quadrupled, would not suffice. This means that while Kritoboulos very much needs the art of increasing his wealth, Socrates does not need it at all. Socrates had very small wants; he thought that the closer a man approaches the divine, the fewer needs he has.[2] He thought, in other words, that to need the art of increasing one's household bespeaks a

[2] *Mem.* I.6.10.

defect, or that that art is needed by more or less inferior men. Before the definition of household management was used for examining Socrates, the successful practitioner of that art seemed to be the free man, the man in no way enslaved by low desires, not to say by prejudices of any kind. We see now that this high view of the economic art was based on the abstraction from "Socrates." That abstraction characteristically went together with the abstraction from justice.

Kritoboulos is so much in need of additional wealth because of what is expected of him. In the first place, as Socrates tells him, he is compelled to offer large sacrifices frequently, for otherwise neither gods nor men will bear with him. We must apply this remark to Socrates, since Xenophon does not do it for us: Socrates is at most compelled to offer small sacrifices rarely.[3] Socrates enumerates next a considerable number of other expensive obligations which Kritoboulos must fulfill— obligations from which, as we must understand, Socrates is altogether free. For instance, Kritoboulos must benefit his fellow citizens lest he lack allies. What crowns all is the fact that despite his desperate need for serious exercise of the economic art, Kritoboulos has not even taken the trouble to acquire that art but applies his mind to frivolous things. It is obvious that Kritoboulos does not belong to the slaves spoken of in the first chapter, if only for the reason that those slaves are men who already possess the economic art. After thus having held up a mirror to Kritoboulos, Socrates returns for a moment to his own case. He grants now that what he possesses might not always be sufficient for his needs, i.e., that he might be com-

---

[3] Cf. *Mem.* I.1.2 and I.3.3. This may throw some light on the cock which Socrates—still?—owed to Asclepius on the day of his death; even this cock he owed only together with Kriton and perhaps Kritoboulos (cf. *Phaedo* 118a7–8 with 59b7).

pelled from time to time to increase his possessions. But this does not compel him to learn the art of increasing his wealth, for, as Kritoboulos knows, there are those who would come to Socrates' help. We must connect this with the result of an earlier exchange between Socrates and Kritoboulos according to which friends too are money: part of Socrates' wealth consists of Kritoboulos and Kriton. Friends are supposed to help one another: Socrates helps Kriton and Kritoboulos with speeches, while Kriton helps Socrates with more tangible things if and when he needs them. This however means that in his way Socrates possesses the art of increasing his wealth. Accordingly, that art belongs to the best life.

It is with a view to these two things that Kritoboulos at once asks Socrates to take charge of his affairs. Socrates needs a moment before he can reply. This reply is not surprising: as Kritoboulos knows, Socrates is poor and Kritoboulos is rich. But the way in which he frames the reply is surprising; he speaks in quite exaggerated and therefore ludicrous terms of the effort that Kritoboulos had to make in order to refute Socrates' assertion that Socrates is wealthy; he speaks as if Kritoboulos had to overcome a powerful resistance on the part of Socrates in order to bring to light the truth about Socrates' poverty—whereas, as everyone knows, not only his poverty but his whole life was like an open book for every passer-by to read.[4] Kritoboulos defends himself well against Socrates' objection: Socrates admittedly knows how to increase his wealth, i.e., to make a small surplus from little; he should therefore be able to make a large surplus if much were put at his disposal. Socrates again exaggerates grossly the effort that Kritoboulos had to make earlier in the conversation; he now

[4] Cf. *Mem.* I.i.io.

goes even further than before by speaking of the enormous effort that Kritoboulos had to make in order to prove to Socrates that only such things are wealth or money for a man which he knows how to use—whereas, as we know, the whole effort in this matter was made by Socrates. But now when ascribing to Kritoboulos the core of the argument of the first chapter much more emphatically than ever before, Socrates does not claim that Kritoboulos had to refute him: he claims that he resisted Kritoboulos only when Kritoboulos tried to bring to light the truth about Socrates' life. However this may be, Socrates' second reply suffices for repelling Kritoboulos' demand, although for no other reason than because in making it, Socrates shifts the ground decisively: when claiming to be wealthy, Socrates had spoken of all his possessions (his house, furniture, and so on); now when disclaiming to be an economist, he speaks of his income-producing possessions. He asserts that he has no such possessions; hence he does not know how to produce income and still less how to make a surplus. This may be sufficient for silencing Kritoboulos, but it cannot satisfy us, for it inevitably leads to the consequence that Socrates has no income whatever—no visible or invisible means of support; he must be a parasite, a beggar—in a word, an unjust man. For, as he himself has heard the perfect gentleman Ischomachos say, "He who knows no other money-making art nor is willing to farm obviously intends to live from stealing or robbing or begging, or is altogether irrational" (XX.15). Everyone can see that this view of Socrates is, as people say, "ironical": Socrates was in truth of course not unjust but thoroughly just, and his very visible means of support were, at least in cases of need, his friends—noble men who regarded it a privilege to come to his assistance. Yet the ironical view is not arbitrary. It is even the true view if one abstracts from the Socratic way of life or is ignorant of it, i.e., if one regards the view of the gentle-men, in the common meaning of the term, as the true view.

Kritoboulos has a last refuge left. As Socrates himself had made clear, a man can possess the art of managing households without possessing a household: why not Socrates himself? Socrates replies that he would have had to learn that art by using another man's household, but no one ever put his house-hold at Socrates' disposal; Socrates could at best do a begin-ner's job, with the usual disastrous consequences, at Kritobou-los' household. Kritoboulos is still not satisfied; he has the feeling that Socrates merely shrinks from a hard or unpleasant job. The sequel will indeed show that Socrates possesses, in a manner, the art of household management, at least that part of it which Kritoboulos most urgently needs. For the time being he sets Kritoboulos' mind at rest by promising to set forth to him whatever he knows of the matter: under no circumstances is Socrates the best available teacher of the desired art, but Socrates will show Kritoboulos who the best masters of it are, so that Kritoboulos can become—the god not resisting—a ter-rific money-maker. There is no suggestion that Kritoboulos would have to pay for instruction by the master in question. As will appear in the sequel, Socrates himself learned the art to the extent to which he learned it without paying for the in-struction. Both Socrates' learning and his teaching economy are acts of economy.

In conclusion Socrates makes clear that he has been con-cerned with finding out who the best masters in Athens of every art are. He used a surprising criterion. Once upon a time he observed to his surprise that some practitioners of an art are quite poor and others quite wealthy. As a consequence he thought this fact worthy of investigation. He found that the twofold effect was quite reasonable. For those who do their work carelessly are bunglers, while those who work carefully and earnestly do their work rather quickly, easily, and gainfully. This seems to mean that all arts are forms of money-getting (or that the art of money-getting accompanies all other arts or is the art of arts), and if the art of household management is the art of increasing one's wealth, one ought to prefer that particular art which is most rewarding in terms of money.

▦▦▦▦▦ Socrates' promises (Chapter III)

However much or little Kritoboulos may have understood of what is implied in Socrates' refusal to become the manager of his household, he surely understood that Socrates had promised him something related to household management. He says now that he will not let go of Socrates before he has shown what he has promised in the presence of "these friends here." We do not know whether those friends, one of whom was Xenophon, were as much in need of learning the art of household management as was Kritoboulos. It is possible that one or the other of them was not in need of it at all and did not have the slightest interest in it but had, perhaps for this very reason, the greatest interest in watching Socrates teaching it and looked forward to this amusing spectacle with eager anticipation. A listener of this kind would be no less benefited by the conversation than Kritoboulos himself.

Socrates had promised Kritoboulos to show him the best masters of the economic art, so that he could learn from them. This could mean that the whole company would pay a visit to the most successful merchant, for instance, just as on another occasion Socrates and his friends paid a visit to the beautiful Theodote.[1] But this time they stay where they are. The reason seems to be that the economic art consists of parts and that it is unlikely that a single man is the master of all of them. At any rate, Socrates renders his promise more precise by speaking of some of the parts of the economic art.

The first of the works belonging to household management

[1] *Mem.* III.11.

is the building of houses; some build useless houses while spending much money, whereas others, spending much less, build houses that are perfectly adequate; Socrates promises Kritoboulos that he will show him both kinds of men. He will, then, not simply take Kritoboulos to the masters of that particular branch of household management but will make him discover those masters by himself; or, more cautiously, he will show him both the masters and the bunglers. Thereafter he will proceed to the next item by exhibiting to Kritoboulos the difference between those who have much furniture of the most various kinds but cannot use it when they need it and those who have much less furniture but have it always ready for use. In this case Kritoboulos suggests spontaneously a reason for the difference, but, as Socrates makes clear, Kritoboulos does not know that reason precisely, since he has an insufficient understanding of the difference between at random, or chance, and order. The next subject will be servants, regarding whom Socrates will exhibit a difference similar to that observed in regard to furniture. He promises next to deal with the two opposite kinds of farmers. Here again Kritoboulos suggests a reason and Socrates again corrects him; Kritoboulos is unaware of the fact that there are two kinds of inefficient farmers. Since Kritoboulos does not understand what Socrates means by the second kind—perhaps this too is due to insufficient understanding of the difference between chance and order—Socrates promises to take him to the inefficient farmers of the second kind too, so that by watching them, he can discern the cause of their failure. In the literal sense of the word, Socrates does not "take" Kritoboulos anywhere in the *Oeconomicus*. Hence it could seem that the present conversation of Socrates with Kritoboulos is only the first stage in Kritoboulos' learning under Socrates' guidance the complete art of household management; the later stages would be located wherever the models of the good and the bad practice of the various parts of the art are to be found; the *Oeconomicus* would be deliberately incomplete. It is almost equally possible, however, that Kritoboulos' learning of the art is completed in the present conversation: Socrates might be the always present model of the bad practice of the economic art or at least of some of its parts.

Be this as it may, Kritoboulos modestly wonders whether he will be able to discern the cause in question. Socrates rebukes him for never testing his ability to discern the causes of things of this kind but instead doing all he can to look at comedies and even persuading Socrates with eagerness to join him in this pleasure. We might feel that Socrates, who knew all the time that Kritoboulos neglected his duties, should never have given in to Kritoboulos' importunities. But perhaps he indulged Kritoboulos' wish in order to gain his confidence or his affection and thus increase the likelihood that the young man would listen to him when he would see fit to remind him of his duties. From the theme "comedy" one is easily led to the theme "ridiculous": Kritoboulos wonders whether, by neglecting to learn the art of household management while indulging his love for comedies, he does not appear ridiculous to Socrates; in other words, he wonders whether he, the lover of comedy, will not himself be a subject of comedy; Socrates replies that he will appear much more ridiculous to himself. He then turns abruptly to another subject belonging to household management, namely, the men who are ruined and those who become wealthy through horsemanship. In this case Kritoboulos knows both types, but his seeing them has not made him proficient in the art of becoming wealthy through horsemanship. According to Socrates, this is due to Kritoboulos' merely beholding the two kinds of men, just as he beholds tragedies and comedies in order to derive enjoyment from seeing and hearing; but what is defensible in the case of dramas, Kritoboulos not wishing to become a poet, is quite inappropriate in the case of horsemanship, Kritoboulos being compelled to make use of that art. In this context Socrates almost addresses Kritoboulos "you fool." Mere beholding, as distinguished from practicing, is utterly insufficient for learning any art, with the possible exception of the art of farming.[2] Socrates' reference to the selling (*pōlēsis*) of horses induces Kritoboulos to wonder whether he wants him to break in colts (*pōloi*). Socrates protests strongly against this misunderstanding ("God forbid"): the raising of animals is out of the question. Here Socrates turns again abruptly to another subject belonging to household management, and in fact to the last one mentioned here, the subject of wives. Socrates can exhibit both good and bad managers of their wives. In all preceding cases—there were five of them—he had mentioned the bunglers before the masters; now he reverses that order. That is to say, he returns to the order that he had followed when contrasting his own wealth with Kritoboulos' poverty,[3] or his mastery with Kritoboulos' ineptitude. In the case of the wives Kritoboulos is altogether at a loss to know whether the husband or the wife is responsible if the wife is bad in regard to the increase of the household. Socrates does not hesitate to make the husband responsible: as a rule he is as responsible for the badness of his wife as the shepherd is for the badness of the sheep, unless he has taught her properly the fine and good things. He then compels Kritoboulos to confess the truth—which he can safely do, since he is among friends—that he has completely neglected this part of his duty: one cannot reasonably expect Kritoboulos' wife to be good.

[2] Cf. XVIII.9–10.
[3] Cf. II.2–4 with II.5–8 and II.17–18.

Since Socrates does not volunteer, as on a former occasion,[4] to speak of his own case as well, there nothing remains for Kritoboulos but to ask Socrates whether those who in his opinion have good wives have themselves educated them. Socrates' answer is evasive: find out for yourself. He admits that he is not the most competent husband or human being regarding this subject; he will introduce Kritoboulos to Aspasia, who will set forth all these things to him in a more knowing manner than he can. This promise at any rate is not kept in the *Oeconomicus;* we are permitted to wonder whether it was kept at all. Socrates does not need Aspasia's help in order to speak now in high terms of the contribution that a wife can make to the increase of her husband's household: while as a rule the possessions enter the house through the husband's actions, the expenditure is mostly the wife's business. Socrates concludes with another promise, but this time the promise is conditional: in case Kritoboulos should think that he needs other kinds of knowledge, Socrates believes that he can show him experts in each of them. He does not say in so many words that Kritoboulos might think he needs those other kinds of knowledge for the increase of his wealth.

Socrates promises Kritoboulos to assist him in acquiring knowledge of six subjects belonging to the art of household management; he does not promise him to do this here and now; surely not all promises are kept in the *Oeconomicus.* That book is not an exhaustive or even completely orderly compendium of the art to which it is devoted. The order of the subjects mentioned in Chapter III is not altogether clear. The first three subjects are the house and things within the house,[5] but while farming and horsemanship are practiced outside the house, the place of the wife is surely within the house.

[4] II.2.
[5] The house, the furniture, the servants *(oiketai).*

This is to say nothing of the fact that up to now we have not heard anything about the connection between household management in general and farming and horsemanship in particular. On the other hand, farming, horsemanship, and the wife belong together, not only because Kritoboulos is particularly defective in these three respects but also because these three things circumscribe the situation with which friends of comedies are confronted at the beginning of Aristophanes' *Clouds*. We shall then assume that for the understanding of the *Oeconomicus* one has to consider, not only the subject matter strictly and narrowly understood (household management) and the qualities of the two interlocutors (Socrates and Kritoboulos), but the *Clouds* as well: *the* Socratic discourse is a response to *the* Socratic comedy, a response not altogether without comical traits.

Socrates' speaking of six parts of the art of household management may have made us oblivious of the oneness of that art, of the singleness of the purpose animating it. He counteracts that danger most effectively by considering the wife exclusively as the husband's helper in increasing his wealth.

▨▨▨▨▨ The case for farming—
I (Chapter IV)

Oikonomia has more than one meaning. We naturally disregard here entirely the application of the term to the gods' administering the whole cosmos.[1] "Household management" may mean in the first place both an art which Socrates possesses and an art which he lacks; this difference corresponds to the difference between Socrates' being wealthy and his being poor; we may call the second meaning common (commonsensical) and the first meaning exalted. The common meaning may be narrowed down or rendered more precise so as to designate the art of wealth-increasing or money-making.[2] In that case our model would be the Athenian best at money-making, regardless of whether he is a citizen or a metic and regardless of the quality of the pursuit or pursuits through which he makes his money. But might one not improve on the best Athenian money-maker? The best economist anywhere would be the man who knows how to acquire the greatest amount of wealth —an amount greater than any other man ever acquired—or if he possesses it already, how to preserve it. Crudely stated, the best economist would be the richest man in the world, in the common meaning of the term "rich." That man was the king of Persia.[3] There are two ways of increasing one's wealth, the way of peace and the way of war—the art of peace and the art of war—and the Persian king devotes himself most effectively

[1] *Mem.* IV.3.13.
[2] Cf. II, end.
[3] *Hellenica* VI.1.12; Plato, *Alcibiades* I.123a–c.

to both arts. If the Persian king is then the model for the economist, the economic art would be identical with the kingly art. This conclusion from the common meaning of "household management" is indeed no longer common. It is in its way as exalted as that meaning according to which Socrates is the master economist. One might even wonder whether Socrates' art is not identical with the kingly art: Socrates seemed to think that the kingly art is identical with happiness, and he said that the most noble virtue and the grandest art are the kingly art.[4] But it seems to be more commonsensical, more prudent to suggest that Socrates' virtue and art are different from the kingly virtue and art, i.e., to admit that "household management" has two exalted meanings, and even to distinguish the following two meanings of "household management": one meaning according to which household management includes the art of war, and another according to which it excludes it.

On an earlier occasion we found it convenient to use the un-Xenophontic term "ironical." An ironical statement has at least two meanings, one which is explicit, untrue, and believed by those who do not understand it to express the speaker's opinion, while the other is implicit, true, and expresses the speaker's opinion. The distinction between the explicit and the implicit meanings must not be mistaken for the distinction between the common and the exalted meanings, for both the common and the exalted meanings can be explicit.

For the progress of the conversation between Socrates and Kritoboulos very much depends on how Kritoboulos understands "household management." At the end of the third chapter Socrates had hinted at the possibility that the household manager might need the sciences or arts other than farming,

---

[4] *Mem.* II.1.17, IV.2.11.

horsemanship, and the like. Kritoboulos replies that he could not well use all the arts; Socrates should exhibit to him those arts or sciences which are thought to be most noble and which would be most becoming for him to engage in, as well as the practitioners of those arts; in addition, Socrates should help him as much as he can, through teaching, toward acquiring the arts in question. His hope that Socrates might manage Kritoboulos' household has been abandoned a long time ago. Socrates approves of Kritoboulos' principle of selection: it surely is noble to select the noblest arts, although we have not heard much of the noble in the previous discussion,[5] and nothing at all in the chapter devoted to the definition of the art of household management. He supports his judgment by the fact that "the so-called banausic [illiberal] arts" are infamous and quite plausibly held in utter disrepute by the cities. Their bad reputation is due to the fact that they spoil the bodies of their practitioners, who are compelled to sit still and to stay indoors; some of those arts even demand that their practitioners spend the day at the fire. Through the softening of the bodies the souls too become much weaker. Furthermore, the practitioners of those arts lack the leisure to be of service to their friends and to the city and therefore are reputed to be bad as defenders of their fatherlands. As a consequence, some of the cities, especially those that are reputed to be good at war, do not admit such people to citizenship. As we see, Socrates adapts himself to the needs, or the tastes, of Kritoboulos, i.e., to the pomp he has assumed and his reputation [6] by rejecting the arts which he rejects, with a view to their reputation and to how they are called; for it is hard to see why the practice of smithing, for instance, should make the body soft.

[5] Cf. III.5 and III.11 (and I.23).
[6] II.4.

In order to find out which arts should be chosen by Kritoboulos, Socrates asks him whether it would make sense that
they should be ashamed to imitate the Persian king. This question is in itself not merely rhetorical, but it is indeed merely
rhetorical as long as one looks at things from the point of view
of the noble, in the sense of the resplendent, vulgarly famous
or of high repute, or the pompous. Accordingly, one cannot
leave matters at what "the cities" do or praise but must turn to
what the king of Persia praises or does. Of the Persian king
people say that he believes farming and the art of war belong
to the most noble and most necessary pursuits and that he devotes himself vigorously to these two pursuits. Kritoboulos
knew of course that the king was greatly concerned with the
art of war, but he had never heard of his being concerned also
with farming; he sees at once that the rumor about the king's
concern with farming would be of decisive importance in his
choice of an art, if one could be sure that the rumor corre-
sponded to the truth. Thereupon Socrates tries to prove the
truth of the rumor by starting from the universally held view
according to which the king devotes himself vigorously to actions connected with war; the king needs a large army in order
to control his subjects, to say nothing of his foreign enemies;
but his soldiers need food; the food is supplied by the king's
civil governors, who do their job in the name of the king and
at his command; at least to this extent the king devotes himself
to farming as well as to the art of war, whereas the military
organization of the Persian Empire shows indisputably that the
king devotes himself to the actions connected with war. In
other words, the reader ought to wonder whether the way in
which Socrates proves that the king devotes himself vigorously
to farming is not equally serviceable for proving that the king
devotes himself vigorously to the arts of smithing or shoemak-

ing. Socrates only wonders whether the king does not care as much for farming as for the defense of his country. The affirmative answer might be supported by the facts that the king cares for farming through his civil governors, and for defense through his military governors, and that the civil and military governors supervise one another mutually. The king cares for farming also because otherwise his subjects would not be able to pay him tribute. The facts hitherto mentioned merely prove that the king regards farming as necessary but not that he regards it as noble. Therefore Socrates goes on to show that the king is concerned with farming, if not for its own sake, at least for his own sake; this is proved to some extent by the king's pleasure gardens that are full of all beautiful and good things which the earth will bring forth, and in which he himself spends most of the time when the season of the year does not prevent it. Socrates is as silent about the fact that at least some of the royal pleasure gardens are full of wild animals as about the king's care for the raising of cattle. He continues his praise of farming by contending (*a*) that according to some, the king gives gifts in the first place to those who have excelled in war and then to those who have excelled in regard to the cultivation of the land; and (*b*) that Cyrus, the most famous king, is said to have said once that since he surpasses everyone in regard to both the cultivation of the land and the defense of it, he ought to receive gifts from the farmers and warriors rather than give gifts to them. This story would convince Kritoboulos fully that Cyrus—the most glorious of all Persian kings— was no less proud of what he did in regard to farming than of his quality as a warrior, if he could be sure that the story is true. Socrates is therefore compelled to speak of the contemporary Cyrus, the younger Cyrus. Even of the younger Cyrus, Socrates did not have first-hand knowledge, but Xenophon had, and Xenophon, we remember, was present at the conversation between Socrates and Kritoboulos on household management. The younger Cyrus would not be as great an authority as the first Cyrus. Socrates is therefore compelled to improve somewhat on the younger Cyrus' record [7] and, above all, to conceal as much as possible the fact that the younger Cyrus is not the same individual as the first Cyrus. The transition from the first Cyrus to the second is as smooth as the transition from the *Memorabilia* to the *Oeconomicus* or, if you wish, from Thucydides' *History* to the *Hellenica*. Besides, many Greeks might have found it difficult that a barbarian should be held up as a model for Greeks. Xenophon was therefore compelled to make his Socrates make the greatest contemporary Greek authority—the Spartan Lysander, the victor in the Peloponnesian War—establish the authority of the younger Cyrus. Socrates does this by retelling a story which Lysander himself had once told to a host in Megara; it is not clear whether Socrates knew that story from that Megarian himself or through intermediaries. When Lysander brought Cyrus the gifts from the allies, Cyrus showed him his pleasure garden in Sardis. Lysander, full of admiration for the beauty of the garden, said to Cyrus that while he admired everything that he saw and smelled, he admired still more the man who had measured out and arranged everything for Cyrus. Cyrus, pleased by this remark, told Lysander that he himself had measured and arranged everything and even planted some of the trees. Lysander could hardly believe that Cyrus, most beautifully and splendidly attired as he was, could have planted anything with his own almost royal hands. Yet Cyrus confirmed the truth of what he had said by an oath by Mithras. Thereupon Lysander, as he said to his Megarian host, took Cyrus' right

[7] Cf. IV.19 with *Anabasis* I.9.31 and II.5.39.

hand and said, "You, Cyrus, seem to me to be justly happy, for you are happy while being a good man." One reason why Lysander was so profoundly impressed by Cyrus' agricultural work was that, in Sparta, Lykurgos had forbidden free men to make money in any manner and in particular by farming.[8] While the authority of original Sparta or of Sparta as a city spoke against money-making in any form, i.e., against the activity to which Socrates encourages Kritoboulos, the greatest living Spartan seemed to have shown profound respect for the practice of farming, at least on one outstanding occasion.

We are unable to say whether Lysander was aware of the critique of Sparta that seems to be implicit in what he said to Cyrus; we are surely aware of the critique of Sparta that is implicit in the *Oeconomicus* as a whole. We must also note that Lysander calls Cyrus a good man; he does not call him a perfect gentleman (*kalos kàgathos*). Besides, Lysander obviously admits that a bad man can be happy or that a man can be unjustly happy. His praising Cyrus as happy while he saw him in Sardis reminds us of Solon's refusal to praise Croesus as happy when he saw that very wealthy king in the same city; Solon seems to have been wiser than Lysander.

We conclude that Socrates' first attempt to make a case for farming was not altogether satisfactory. Let us then turn to his second attempt.

[8] *Resp. Lac.* 7.1–3. Cf. Plato, *Republic* 547c6–d9.

The case for farming—
II (Chapter V)

Xenophon achieves Socrates' transition to his second attempt by saying, " 'This, Kritoboulos, *I* narrate,' said Socrates, "because it shows that not even the altogether blessed can abstain from farming.' " The emphatic "I" compels us to wonder whether Socrates' motive for narrating the story of Lysander and Cyrus to Kritoboulos is the same as Lysander's motive for narrating the same story to the Megarian, i.e., whether Lysander narrated it in order to praise farming and encourage it. Socrates goes on to give reasons why not even the altogether blessed can abstain from farming. It seems then that the reason or reasons given in the preceding chapter were not sufficient. The reasons now given are these: "the pursuit of farming seems to be at the same time some soft pleasure, an increase of the household, and a training of the bodies so that they can do whatever befits a free man." Socrates qualifies his praise of farming somewhat by speaking of what the pursuit of farming "seems" to do, but the word for "seeming" which he now uses [1] does not directly refer to what is generally thought to be, to what people say, to opinions, reputation, rumor, hearsay, or authority; references of this kind abounded in the preceding chapter; they are absent from Socrates' long speech in the present chapter. This difference is no doubt due to the fact that in the bulk of the preceding chapter Socrates argued on the basis of the example set by the king of Persia, whereas in the present chapter he is completely silent on Persia. References to

[1] *Eoike*, not *dokei*.

what Socrates knew from hearsay about the Persian king gave occasion for three of the four responses of Kritoboulos.[2] He does not once interrupt Socrates' long speech in the present chapter. The case for farming that Socrates makes without any regard to the Persian king is more didactic or rhetorical[3] and less dialogical than the case he makes with regard to the Persian king.

It is only natural that Socrates should assign the central place among the reasons for farming to the increase of the household, for increase of the household is, as we have learned, the purpose of household management. But "increase of the household" is now flanked and hence limited by two other ends. The qualification of increase of the household by another consideration was begun in the preceding chapter, when Kritoboulos proposed that Socrates select for him, not the most lucrative art or arts, but the arts that are reputed to be most noble. In the present chapter the concern with nobility (beauty, being honored) is abandoned in favor, in the first place, of the concern with pleasure.[4] The pleasant seems to be the most obvious alternative to the noble. Why is Socrates concerned with such an alternative? What is pleasant, and in particular what is pleasant to the body, is more independent of opinion and reputation than what is noble. Yet it is obvious that a man striving for pleasure without any qualification whatever would not choose farming; the central argument in Socrates' long speech[5] indicates the price one has to pay for

[2] IV.5, IV.12, IV.14, IV.17.

[3] Cf. especially the eight rhetorical questions in V.8–10.

[4] V.2, V.3, V.9, V.10, V.11. Cf. especially V.3 with IV.23. Regarding "honor," see especially *Hiero* 7.

[5] The speech consists of five arguments; their beginnings are indicated by "first" (V.2), "then" (V.3), "then" (V.3), "then" (V.5), and "furthermore" (V.12).

the pleasures derived from farming (sacrifices and hard work). After having spoken of the pleasure that farming affords especially to the wife, but also to the servants, the children, and the friends, Socrates says that it seems strange to him that a free human being might possess a more pleasant possession than a farm or discover a more pleasant pursuit than farming; he no longer speaks of a free man (*anēr*); a free man may know of greater pleasures than those connected with farming.[6]

The concern with nobility as distinguished from pleasure is to some extent preserved in the concern with the "training of the bodies so that they can do whatever befits a free man." Socrates had in fact spoken of this concern when replying to Kritoboulos' question at the beginning of the preceding chapter. But since the guiding consideration there was that of the noble, he was compelled to go beyond "the cities" toward the king of Persia. Accordingly, he had not even mentioned freedom or free human beings, let alone free men, in the preceding chapter; in Persia there are no free men but only slaves and a single master.[7] The free man as presented in the present chapter is both a farmer and a warrior, whereas in the preceding chapter the farmers and the warriors were presented as two separate parts of the subjects of the Persian king. Farming is now said to make good soldiers, both hoplites and knights. The teaching of the present chapter, combined with the teaching of the beginning of the preceding chapter, is to the effect that farmers are better soldiers than craftsmen or, in other words, that if the farmers and the craftsmen were enrolled in opposed military units, the farmers would easily defeat the craftsmen.[8] Given the separation in Persia of the soldiers and the farmers, we must draw the further conclusion that in Persia the soldiers

[6] Cf. *Hiero* 7.3–4.

[7] *Anabasis* I.9.29; *Hellenica* VI.1.12. Cf. Aristotle, *Nichomachean Ethics* 1160b27–29.

[8] Consider VI.6–7.

keep down the farmers with ease; the reasonable praise of peasant soldiers must not make us oblivious of the virtues of professional soldiers.[9] The praise of the farmer-soldier is a praise of the citizen-soldier. Accordingly, Socrates says now that farming—or rather the earth—teaches justice, though not to all men, whereas he had been completely silent on justice in the "Persian" chapter: transcending the city means transcending justice. Given the connection between justice and piety, we ought not to be surprised to observe that the "Persian" chapter, which is silent on justice, is silent also on piety or the gods, while the present chapter, which mentions justice, speaks more than once of the gods.[10] It is true that in the Persian chapter there occur three oaths, while not a single oath occurs in the present chapter. But the absence of oaths from a speech is not a sign of its lacking piety or even of its lacking gravity, and vice versa. "The earth, being a goddess, teaches justice to those who are able to learn, for she gives the most goods in return to those who serve her best." At the same time "the earth stimulates in some degree the farmers to armed protection of the country by nourishing her crops in the open for the strongest to take": the earth also encourages the right of the stronger, i.e., what looks very much like injustice. More cautiously stated, there is a close kinship between the art of farming and the art of war, a kinship which induces Socrates to abstain from calling the art of farming a peaceable art.[11]

Another difference between the two chapters is that the Persian chapter is silent on beasts, whereas the following chapter has not a little to say about them.[12] This is connected with

[9] Cf. the reference to mercenary soldiers in the "Persian" chapter, IV.6.

[10] V.3, V.4, V.10; cf. *Anabasis* III.2.13.

[11] V.7, V.12–16. Cf. I.17 and VI.1.

[12] V.3, V.5, V.6. Consider the distinction made in V.3 between the *phyein* of vegetation and the *trephein* of animals; cf. V.18 and VI.10.

the fact that in Chapter V, Socrates speaks of both the earth and farming, and hence of the difference between them,[13] i.e., of the difference between something natural and an art. The fact that the earth rather than farming nourishes the crops in the open for the strongest to take therefore throws some light on the complex relation between nature and justice.

Socrates' twofold case for farming, but especially his long and uninterrupted speech,[14] left Kritoboulos without any objection except that in farming men cannot foresee the outcome: however careful and thoughtful the farmer may have been, the weather may ruin his crops and diseases may ruin his cattle. In his reply Socrates makes a point which he might not have made but for Kritoboulos' objection: [15] the gods are the decisive lords in farming no less than in warfare; just as prior to warlike actions men appease the gods and consult them by means of sacrifices and omens as to what men should do or forbear to do, men must also appease and worship the gods in regard to agricultural actions. Socrates thus intimates what is perhaps the deepest reason for the kinship between farming and warfare, or for the difference between the arts of farming and war on the one hand and all other arts on the other hand, while alluding to the difference between the two arts in the demands they make on piety. We may also say that while hitherto he has merely presupposed that piety is good, or at least necessary, he now proves it.

[13] Cf. V.5: the wild beasts are nourished by the earth; the horse is nourished by farming. Cf. also V.11.

[14] Cf. the beginning of V.18: "After having heard this, Kritoboulos said . . . ."

[15] Cf. the beginning of V.19: "After having heard this, Socrates said . . . ."

🀀🀀🀀🀀🀀 A simplifying retrospect and a complicating prospect (Chapter VI)

Socrates had said that the peculiarly hazardous character of warfare and of farming makes it necessary for us to appease and to worship the gods. Kritoboulos approves of this view yet speaks of warfare and peace. He arrives, therefore, at the demand that we ought to begin every work with the gods' help, or at the view suggested by the Socrates of the *Memorabilia* [1] that the art dealing with what is most important in every art, namely, with the ultimate beneficial or harmful outcome of the artisan's activity, or the art of arts, is the art of divination. Kritoboulos, who is pleased at now knowing, thanks to Socrates, better than before what he must do in order to earn his living, now asks Socrates to try to complete his account of household management by starting at the point where he had left off. It is safe to say that he regarded Socrates' statement on the need for piety as belonging, not to the art of household management itself, but rather, as we said, to the art of arts. But we cannot exclude the possibility that in Kritoboulos' view other parts also of Socrates' previous speeches do not belong to the art of household management. At any rate Socrates proposes that they recapitulate what they had agreed upon, and the recapitulation that follows differs strikingly from the conversation it is meant to summarize.

A recapitulation is a kind of repetition. In a good author who as such is not prolix, a repetition is never a mere repetition and very rarely a literal repetition; in a good author a rep-

[1] I.1.6–9.

etition always teaches us something we could not have learned from the first statement. The most striking examples of repetitions in Xenophon's writings are these: some of the definitions given in *Memorabilia* III.8–9 are "repeated" in IV.6; the last chapter of the *Memorabilia* is "repeated" in the *Apology of Socrates;* large parts of the *Hellenica* are "repeated" in the *Agesilaos.*

According to Socrates' proposal, the recapitulation of what they had agreed upon hitherto should provide them with a model for their procedure with the rest of the subject matter. Kritoboulos compares the pleasure that they who are associated in speeches derive from going over their speeches in which they agree, with the pleasure that men who are associated in money matters derive from going over their accounts without getting into dispute. One may doubt whether businessmen always derive pleasure from their agreeing about their being bankrupt, i.e., whether Kritoboulos is sufficiently earnest about money-making. He surely holds that partnership in speeches resembles partnership in money-making. If there is such a resemblance, one is tempted to go on toward holding that the art of money-making is an image of the art of conversing or reasoning, or that the art of money-making, and not the art of divination, is the art accompanying all arts or is the art of arts. It is safe to say that the art of divination is not an image of the art of reasoning. But if the art of money-making accompanies all other arts much less ambiguously than does the art of divination, it would not be surprising that *the* Socratic discourse is devoted to the art of increasing one's wealth. Still, the remark that tempted us into this consideration is made by Kritoboulos, and we do not know what Socrates thought of it.

In his recapitulation Socrates repeats in the first place the chief result of their joint attempt to define household management. If possible, Socrates is now still more silent on the justice or legality of the acquisition of wealth than he was in Chapter I. It should be added that he remains silent on justice, piety, and legality throughout the recapitulation. He is also silent about the fact that household management includes the management of one's wife. Thereafter he restates the case for farming with scrupulous omission of anything reminding one of the Persian king; this omission might be the direct consequence of the decision to recapitulate only those things on which Socrates and Kritoboulos had agreed. Socrates is completely silent about the self-examination of Kritoboulos and Socrates in regard to their managing their households, about everything which could possibly remind one of Aristophanes, and about Socrates' promises. On the other hand, he claims that they had said things about the farmer-soldier as the citizen-soldier par excellence about which they had not said a word but which helped us to a better understanding of the difference between Persia and "the cities." Above all—and this in a way compensates for the silence on Persia—he claims that they had agreed about farming being a work and a science very fit for a perfect gentleman, one of their reasons allegedly being that farming seems to be the science most easy to learn. In a word, in the recapitulation Socrates not only introduces the theme "the perfect gentleman," but he does everything in his power to strengthen his recommendation of farming to the perfect gentleman.

Kritoboulos is now fully convinced that farming is preferable from every point of view (from that of the noble, that of the good, and that of the pleasant) to any other way of making a living. He is now eager to hear the causes why some farmers are highly successful and others fail altogether—causes which Socrates had claimed he had learned. He thus reminds

Socrates of one of the promises he had made to him in Chapter III; that promise was the only one accompanied by Socrates' rebuke of Kritoboulos for his deplorable propensity to prefer comedies to farming.

Socrates proposes to fulfill his earlier promise or to grant Kritoboulos' present request by narrating to him from the beginning how he had once come together with a man who seemed to him truly to belong to the kind of men who are justly called perfect gentlemen. "Perfect gentleman" is the ordinary English translation of a Greek expression which more literally translated means "a man who is noble [beautiful, fair, fine] and good." Socrates was apparently puzzled about the meaning of the juxtaposition of "beautiful" and "good." Before he knew what a "beautiful and good man" is, he had discovered with ease what good makers of beautiful things (e.g., good builders and good painters) are; so he wondered what kind of beautiful things, or what kind of things, are produced by the perfect gentleman, and his soul desired very much to come together with one of these men. But in the case of the perfect gentleman, not the product, but the man himself, is called beautiful; Socrates was therefore for a while misled into believing that a perfect gentleman is a man who is beautiful to look at; yet he found that some men beautiful to look at were quite depraved in their souls. He decided therefore to take his bearings, not by sight but by hearing, by reputation: he decided to try to come together with a man who was universally called a perfect gentleman. That man was Ischomachos.

Socrates thus brings about a shift from "household management" to "perfect gentlemanship"; the question is no longer what the work of household management is but what the work of the perfect gentleman is.[2] It is an important shift, although

[2] Cf. VI.13–14 with I.2.

it was prepared by Kritoboulos' desire to hear of the lucrative science which is reputed to be most noble or beautiful. After Socrates has made perfect gentlemanship the theme, we understand better than before why the *Oeconomicus* is *the* Socratic dialogue. For, as we know, Socrates was exclusively concerned with ethics and politics, with virtue and the city, and "perfect gentlemanship" includes in a manner all ethical and political themes.[3] Yet we cannot conceal from ourselves the fact that in the *Oeconomicus* perfect gentlemanship is approached from an angle which is not the most gentlemanly one, from a point of view which is rather low: from the point of view of the question of how the perfect gentleman earns his living; we view the perfect gentleman primarily, not in his splendor, but in his needs. Farming, the science or art most befitting the gentleman, was repeatedly said to fulfill the most fundamental need of all human beings, the need for food.[4]

By the manner in which Socrates is about to fulfill one of his promises he achieves another change that is not unimportant. Hitherto we have listened to his conversing as an older man with a younger man; we perceived him, let us say, as an oldish man. From now on we shall hear him bringing to light and life a unique event of his past. That event was his discovery of what perfect gentlemanship is. There was, then, a time when Socrates, no longer a child, did not know what perfect gentlemanship is, when his thought had not yet aspired to the height on which perfect gentlemen dwell. More precisely, there was a time when Socrates, no longer a child, had not yet knowingly met a single perfect gentleman.

Xenophon narrates to his readers Socrates' conversation with Kritoboulos. The largest part of this narrative consists of Soc-

[3] *Mem.* I.1.16.
[4] IV.4, IV.15, V.2, V.17.

rates' narrating to Kritoboulos his conversation with Ischomachos. In this part of the *Oeconomicus* the narrator Xenophon
disappears completely, or almost completely, behind the narrator Socrates.[5] We would be entitled to call this part of the
dialogue *the* Socratic discourse par excellence, were it not for
the fact that in it Socrates is most visibly the pupil. Since from
now on Kritoboulos does nothing but listen to Socrates' narrative of an earlier conversation, he has no opportunity to approve or to disapprove of what he hears. At least we have no
means of knowing how he was affected by Socrates' tale, just
as we have no means of knowing how Hiero was affected by
Simonides' praise of benevolent tyranny.

[5] The only exception occurs in X.1.

▣▣▣▣▣ *Gynaikologia—I:* Marriage according to the gods and according to the law (Chapter VII)

It was not easy for Socrates to have his unique conversation with Ischomachos, for Ischomachos seldom had the required leisure. The conversation was rendered possible by the lucky accident—lucky at any rate for Socrates and his friends—that Ischomachos had an appointment in town with strangers who stood him up. Thus it came about that Socrates once saw him sitting in the colonnade of Zeus the Deliverer—the deliverer of the Greeks in particular from the Persian danger [1]—and sat down by his side. He told him without beating around the bush that he would like to hear from him where he spends his time and what he does in order to be called a perfect gentleman. Ischomachos laughed at Socrates' straightforward and unusual question but was pleased by the implied compliment. He is not aware, he replied, how people call him in his absence, but at any rate in important or official business they call him distinctly, not the perfect gentleman (for there are quite a few of them in Athens), but Ischomachos with his patronymic. (Ischomachos does not tell Socrates his father's name. Hence we do not know distinctly which of the many Athenians called Ischomachos enlightened Socrates about perfect gentlemanship.) Ischomachos never squanders his time indoors. To apply to him what Xenophon says, with some exaggeration,[2] of Socra-

---

[1] *Lyra Graeca*, ed. J. M. Edmonds (London: W. Heinemann, 1922–1927), Simonides fragment 169.

[2] Cf. *Mem.* III.10–11 and IV.2.

tes, he is always in the open. But whereas Socrates spends all his time in the promenades, the gymnasia, and the market place, Ischomachos ordinarily spends all his time on his farm.[3] If Ischomachos' way of life is that of the perfect gentleman, we are then compelled to conclude that Socrates was not a perfect gentleman: the perfect gentleman is seldom entirely at leisure,[4] whereas Socrates is so most of the time.

Ischomachos' outdoor life, in contrast to that of Socrates, is connected with the fact that he is emphatically a man, an *hombre* (*anēr*): his indoor affairs are well taken care of by his wife. His remark to this effect has the consequence that his management of his wife—and, in the first place, his education of her—becomes the first subject of Socrates' conversation with him. No doubt that remark would not have had that effect if it had not excited Socrates' curiosity as strongly as it did: Socrates is more pleased to hear Ischomachos narrating how he began teaching his wife than to hear him narrating the most resplendent athletic or equestrian contest; he is more pleased to contemplate the virtue of a living woman than to look at the portrait by Zeuxis of a beautiful woman.[5] (Socrates does not say of course that he prefers Ischomachos' narrative of how he educated his wife to a comedy.) On no other occasion does Socrates in the *Oeconomicus* express his eagerness to learn in such strong terms, although the primary purpose of his conversation with Ischomachos was to find out what perfect gentlemanship is. He does not say why he is so excited about the theme "the wife." Was he not yet married but contemplating marriage and eager to get the best guidance for his venture in the most convenient or unobtrusive manner? Or was he al-

[3] Cf. VI.10 with *Mem.* I.1.10.
[4] VII.1. Cf. Aristotle, *Eth. Nic.* 1177b4 ff.
[5] VII.9, X.1.

ready married to Xanthippe but a bungler at taming her? [6]
This much is certain: the Socrates who conversed with Ischomachos had no inkling of the state of knowledge, or rather
ignorance, in which nice and sweet Athenian [7] girls entered
marriage,[8] just as he did not know what a perfect gentleman
is. Ischomachos surely leaves no doubt about his wife's having
been a nice or sweet bride.[9]

Almost the whole education of which she could boast, she
owed to her husband. Before beginning to educate her, he of-
fered sacrifice and prayer together with her, thus complying
with the rule laid down by the Socrates of the *Memorabilia*
and by Kritoboulos that one ought to begin every work with
appeasing the gods. At Socrates' request Ischomachos speaks
first of his first conversation with his wife that was devoted to
teaching her, in the serious sense of teaching, i.e., of a being together consisting entirely of conversation. The account given
by Ischomachos is not meant to be a verbatim account. He
speaks from memory.[10] When telling his story to Socrates, he
was already married for some time. At the beginning of the
first lesson he explained to his wife the purpose for which they
married. That purpose was obviously not "sleeping together"

[6] Cf. *Symp.* 2.10.

[7] As for the difference in upbringing between Athenian and Spartan
girls, cf. VII.6 with *Resp. Lac.* 1.3–4.

[8] Socrates shows himself well informed on this subject in his conversation with Kritoboulos, III.12–13. Ivo Bruns, *Das literarische Portrait der
Griechen* (Berlin, 1896), p. 423, notes that Socrates, in *Oeconomicus* XI
ff., "raises questions more frequently and in greater detail" than in Chapters VII–X, where his questions are more like those of "a man who
hears about things really new to him."

[9] A "timid fawn-like creature," according to Dakyns on VII.10 (*The
History of Xenophon*, trans. Henry G. Dakyns [New York: Tandy-
Thomas, 1909]).

[10] VII.9, VII.10, VII.43, end.

but the enjoyment of the community of the household and of children. Since they could not yet have children, he postponed the deliberation about the children's education until the proper time; but he already stated then that the children, as well as the household, are to be a common good for husband and wife, since the children are to be the best allies of the parents and their support in old age. The fact that Ischomachos did not instruct his wife on the education of children in his first conversation with her does not explain, however, why the *Oeconomicus* does not contain a section devoted to the management of children, for considerable time must have elapsed between that conversation and Ischomachos' conversation with Socrates. Besides, Socrates himself was a father and could as such be expected to guide Kritoboulos in this awesome sphere, unless one were to say that he was not a model of a father. Be this as it may, at present at any rate, the newly wedded couple must limit itself to keeping what it has in as good a condition as possible and to increasing its household by noble and just means, as Ischomachos suggests to his wife. In the conversation between Socrates and Ischomachos which takes place, as it were, under the auspices of Zeus the Deliverer, the purpose of household management is then declared to be, not simply increase of the household, but only its noble and just increase. It is therefore all the more remarkable that in Socrates' conversation with Kritoboulos which took place at a later, perhaps at a much later, date, and especially in the definition therein given of household management, this explicit limitation does not occur.[11]

Since Ischomachos' wife does not see how she could contribute anything toward the increase of their wealth, he urges her to do as well as she can what the gods have enabled her to

[11] In the Ischomachos section, as distinguished from the Kritoboulos section, Socrates is the first to swear.

do by bringing her forth, and what in addition the law praises. It is not surprising that immediately after the limitation of the increase of wealth to its noble and just increase, the law should make its first appearance in the *Oeconomicus*. As the phrasing shows, Ischomachos does not ascribe divine origin to the law. Nor does he mean by law merely the law laid down by the Athenian legislator. With a view to his later references to law,[12] we may say that the law which he has in mind is an unwritten law, traces of which are found in a variety of codes and of whose origin nothing is known except that it is not divine. What the gods have generated,[13] what owes its being to the gods, is "nature" as distinguished in particular from law. "Nature" and "law" make their first appearance in the *Oeconomicus* in the same context, in the same chapter.[14]

To counteract his wife's extreme modesty or diffidence, Ischomachos first tries to reassure her by comparing the wife's position in the household to the position of the queen bee in the beehive. This comparison is obviously liable to misunderstanding and even to misuse, if one does not know first the peculiar function of the female human being, and one cannot know this without some understanding of the function of the female in all animal species. Ischomachos therefore speaks first of why the gods coupled together females and males in all animal species and in particular in the human species (VII.18–29), and then of what the law does to join together husband and wife (VII.30–31), in order to take up thereafter the comparison of the wife with the queen bee.

Ischomachos sets forth three judicious considerations of the gods, which, it seems to him, induce them to couple together the female and the male chiefly in order that the community

12 XIV.4–7.
13 *Ephysan.*
14 VII.16, VII.22.

may be as useful as possible to the two: (1) The coupling together serves the purpose of procreation, i.e., the preservation of the species of animals. (2) In the case of the human species, at any rate, the union serves the purpose of providing for the parents' support in their old age. (3) Men, as distinguished from the beasts, cannot spend their whole life in the open air but also need shelter; hence they need both indoor and outdoor work—hence the twofold rulership supplied by the wife on the one hand and the husband on the other. Ischomachos speaks at length only of the third consideration.[15] Speaking like a teacher and therefore, in the circumstances, somewhat ponderously, he explains to his bride, who was perhaps not as ignorant as he assumed, that the necessaries of life must be procured through outdoor work but must then be transformed into food and clothing by indoor work, to say nothing of other necessary activities which are properly performed indoors. We might completely forget that we are listening to Socrates' narrating his conversation with Ischomachos, i.e., we might believe that the lessons are given by Socrates or by Xenophon, if Xenophon (or Socrates) did not remind us from time to time of the context;[16] for when reading, "I said, 'O woman . . . , we must . . . ,'" we might think that Socrates tells us what he had said to his wife, or we might even think that Ischomachos is addressing Socrates "O woman."[17] Ac-

---

[15] As for the central consideration, cf. Democritus (Hermann Diels-Walther Kranz, *Die Fragmente der Vorsokratiker* [7th ed.; Berlin: Weidmann, 1934-1937]), B 275-278, A 166, A 169, A 170.

[16] "He [Ischomachos] said that he had said [to his wife]" (VII.18, 23, 30); "[he had said that] he had said" (VII.22).

[17] Cf. Xenophon's silence on Socrates' manliness. In the *Symposion* (9.1) Lykon says to Socrates, "By Hera, O Socrates, you seem to me to be a fair and good human being"; Socrates had spoken shortly before of the true *andragathia*.

cording to Ischomachos, who, in contradistinction to Socrates, is silent about *eros* in marriage and in particular about the gods' particular kindness to men in not limiting their sexual pleasures to special seasons of the year,[18] it was with a view to the difference between indoor and outdoor work that the god fashioned the nature of the woman and also of her counterpart; he modestly supplies this explanation with an "it seems to me." By shaping the man's and the woman's bodies and souls differently, it likewise seems to Ischomachos, the gods prescribed or enjoined to them their different occupations. He denies that woman is designed to be more temperate than man. Nor does he assert that the law enjoins greater temperance on her than on the man. Or was this not a suitable subject for the first conversation? At any rate, according to Ischomachos there is perfect agreement between nature and law: the law puts the stamp of the noble on the specific actions for which the god has designed the two sexes; to stay indoors is noble for the wife and base for the husband. The law that Ischomachos has in mind is effective through praising (and blaming) rather than through coercing or punishing; if a man acts against the divine or natural order by neglecting his work or doing that of the wife, his disorderly conduct is perhaps noticed by the gods and he is punished for it.[19] Ischomachos is less certain of the gods' omniscience than is Socrates.[20]

Accordingly, when he turns eventually to the queen bee, he says that that animal too "seems" to him to do the work that the god prescribed to it. At this point his wife, who had listened in silence and perhaps in awe to her husband's lecture on

[18] *Mem.* I.4.7, I.4.12.
[19] Contrast VII.16 and VII.30 with *Hiero* 3.9. Cf. *Anabasis* II.6.16–20. Cf. *Resp. Lac.* 3.4.
[20] *Mem.* I.1.19.

the different functions of females and males in general and of human females and males in particular, asks him what kind of work done by the queen bee can be compared to the work she is supposed to do; the teaching, which now ceases altogether to be theological,[21] becomes again dialogical, at least till the end of the chapter. Ischomachos replies that the wife can be compared to the queen bee since both control even the out-door work of the members of the community while they themselves always stay indoors. The queen bee does not suffer the bees to be idle; Ischomachos is silent here on the drones. There are two reasons for this silence: (1) the well-ordered household does not tolerate human drones; (2) Ischomachos rejects the drones proper as useless (XVII.14) and hence does not see why, and even whether, the god has fashioned them. Needless to say, Ischomachos' comparison of the two kinds of females is apt in many points, although not all of them are im-mediately convincing to his bride. For instance, the queen bee controls the upbringing of the progeny, and when the young ones are fit to work, she sends them out under a leader to found a colony; the wife apparently wonders whether she is to send out her children after they have grown up, to found a colony under a leader other than herself (or her husband); Is-chomachos must therefore tell her that he was thinking not of her children but of those of the servants who are to be sent out by her to work in the fields. Furthermore, it is not clear whether Ischomachos believes that the queen bee takes care of the sick bees as the good wife takes care of the sick servants; he is surely delighted at his wife's seeing at once that this kind of work is most rewarding, since it makes the servants grateful and enhances their good will; returning to the image of the

[21] Gods are no longer mentioned in VII.33–43. A kind of compensa-tion for this is supplied by the wife's two "by Zeus" (VII.37, VII.40).

queen bee, he says that the bees become so attached to the queen bee who takes care of them that when she leaves the hive, none thinks of staying behind, but all follow her; one wonders whether in the case of divorce all servants will leave together with the wife. Above all, the comparison of the wife with the queen bee suffers from the fact that it does not provide a proper place for the husband and master. Ischomachos saves the comparison as well as he can by surreptitiously admitting that his wife is indeed the ruler of the maidservants rather than of the menservants and by stating powerfully and movingly that if she proves to be manifestly superior to him, she will be the mistress of him who is the direct ruler of the menservants, even and especially after she has ceased to be young and of youthful bloom.

ạạạạạ *Gynaikologia—II:* Order, I
(Chapter VIII)

In the preceding chapter it had taken some time until the dialogue between Ischomachos and Socrates disappeared completely or almost completely behind the dialogue between Ischomachos and his wife, or rather behind Ischomachos' lecture to his wife. Yet one could say that it was Socrates who steered Ischomachos toward the subject of that lecture. The situation is different in the present chapter. At its beginning Socrates asks Ischomachos whether he had observed that his instruction had been in any way successful. After an emphatic, if perfunctory, "Yes, by Zeus," Ischomachos turns at once to another subject on which, he says, he instructed his wife or lectured to her. That subject came up without any contrivance on Ischomachos' part. His wife could not find something belonging to her sphere which he wanted. She was vexed; she blushed deeply; she was annoyed with herself. So he had first to comfort her. He did this especially by making himself responsible for her failure: he had failed to instruct her about the virtue of order. Even this initial exchange between the spouses is not presented as an exchange of words, as a dialogue, although it was one; in the rest of the chapter Ischomachos addresses his wife four time with "O wife" but she never says a word; he once addresses Socrates with "O Socrates," but Socrates never says a word. One may trace the wife's silence safely to her modesty reinforced by her feeling of shame about her failure; one cannot thus explain Socrates' silence.

The theme of Ischomachos' second lecture is the usefulness

and beauty of order for human beings. He gives three examples: a chorus, an army, and a warship. He speaks briefly about the chorus, and in the central place and much more extensively about the army. There may be two reasons for this preference: choruses consist exclusively of human beings, whereas both households and armies consist of human beings, beasts, and artifacts; and Ischomachos may be more a military man than a music man. There is this further difference between a well-ordered chorus and a well-ordered army: a well-ordered chorus is enjoyable to see and to hear for everybody, whereas a well-ordered army is useful and pleasant to look at for friends and harmful and painful to look at for enemies. Furthermore, armies are well ordered so as to be able to reduce enemy armies to disorder or confusion. This is to say nothing of the military worth of "irregulars." Order, it seems, belongs to rest rather than to motion. No doubt there can be well-ordered motions, as is shown in particular by a fast-marching army or a fast-sailing warship, but in these cases, at any rate, order prevails only as long as the motions have not yet reached their climax; every battle, however victorious at the end, abounds in confusion and disharmonious sounds. Nevertheless, the two examples are not altogether inept: the manager of the household, despite the peaceful character of his pursuit, is in need of allies whom he would not need if managing one's household, i.e., increasing one's wealth, were not also a kind of war.[1] Ischomachos is properly silent about the inevitable confusion of battles. Instead he speaks of easily avoidable and in every respect absurd kinds of disorder of which a farmer might become guilty; he then turns to admonishing his wife to join him in putting all their belongings into their proper places so that they will be always available for use.

[1] II.5; cf. *Mem.* III.4.10.

Ischomachos is not quite satisfied with the three examples of order which he has given. Once upon a time he had seen the most beautiful and most accurate order of utensils on a great Phoenician merchantman. The example is most apt, because a merchantman is neither a music nor a primarily warlike thing, or, more precisely, because Ischomachos is concerned with instructing his wife in how to establish and keep order among their implements or utensils.[2] He was already married at the time he had that experience, for he spoke of it immediately afterward to his wife. Now when setting out to recount it to Socrates, he addresses him by name: the example of order which he is about to present is to instruct, to educate even Socrates. On the merchantman Ischomachos saw a great variety of kinds of implements well ordered with a view to immediate use in difficult and even terrifying circumstances; the very survival of everyone aboard depended on the optimal use being made of the small space available and therefore on the most beautiful and most accurate order. This requires the utmost care, especially on the part of the man in charge, as Ischomachos found out when he observed the boatswain, who already possessed perfect knowledge of where everything was placed and how much there was of it, inspecting everything as to its being handy in every situation that might arise. When he asked him why he did this, the boatswain told him that there is no time to search for the needed things when the god raises a storm at sea, for the god threatens and punishes the slack; one must be satisfied when the god does not destroy those who do no wrong; when he saves those who do service very well, one must be grateful to the gods. Ischomachos, who reports the Phoenician boatswain's view of the god and the gods, finds no fault with it; as for Socrates, he is silent throughout the chap-

2 VIII.11, VIII.23.

ter. The boatswain is more certain than Ischomachos about the gods punishing (and therefore noticing) the slack. On the other hand, he is as doubtful as Ischomachos about evil befalling only the bad, i.e., about whether one can speak in strict parlance of divine punishment. In the boatswain's statement, and hence in the whole chapter, order is not presented as in any way rooted in something divine; it is presented rather as being altogether of human origin; the gods are mentioned only as disturbers of order.[3] One could say that order is presented here as devised against the unpredictable actions of the gods.

Ischomachos' story of the Phoenician merchantman and its boatswain reminds us of Socrates' story of Cyrus and his pleasure garden. In both cases barbarians are presented as models in regard to order. In both cases the order is of human origin. Yet in the Persian story the ordered thing is the pleasure garden, and the orderer is a man who was almost a king; in the Phoenician story the ordered thing is a merchantman, and the orderer is a nameless boatswain. In the Persian story the order belongs together with Cyrus' resplendent adornments of all kinds; in the Phoenician story the splendor is altogether replaced by utility.[4] Ischomachos tells his story on the basis of what he himself had seen on the merchantman and heard from the boatswain; Socrates, however, had not seen Cyrus' pleasure garden or talked with Lysander and still less with Cyrus, and perhaps not even with the Megarian to whom Lysander told the story. Since Socrates heard Ischomachos' story directly from him, one could say that in the case of the Phoenician story Socrates is closer to the original than in the case of the

[3] Cf. XVII.4. The relative silence on the gods is not compensated in Chapter VIII by any oaths (cf. above, Chapter VII, n. 21). The oath in VIII.1 precedes the discussion of order.

[4] Cf. Socrates' identification of the beautiful or noble with the good in *Mem.* III.8.5–7; cf. *Mem.* IV. 6.8–9. Cf. Plato, *Republic* 458e4.

Persian story. The Persian story is silent on the gods, although it is adorned with an oath; the opposite is true of the Phoenician story. There can be no doubt that Socrates has, so to speak, nothing in common with the Phoenician boatswain, whereas he has very much to do with Ischomachos, the model gentleman, and with Cyrus, the model ruler. We must therefore wonder whether in his view Ischomachos or Cyrus occupies the higher rank. We must leave it open whether the contrasts just pointed out are of any use for settling this issue.

After having presented the most revealing example of order, Ischomachos turns again to admonishing his wife. He states to her in a very clear and forceful manner the lesson he had learned through seeing the exact order prevailing on the ship rather than through listening to the boatswain. In fact it is not at all certain that he reported to her his conversation with the boatswain. Both the example of the merchantman and the contrast between the conditions to be found on a ship, on the one hand, and in a household, on the other, show how good and easy it is to arrange the household utensils in their proper order. Such arrangement, however, is not only good but beautiful as well. It is a beautiful sight if every kind of thing, however humble, is ranged in rows and separate from other kinds; no grave or solemn man, but only a wit, will laugh at the suggestion that a well-ordered array of pots and pans deserves to be called graceful. Ischomachos, to whom that grave or solemn name "the perfect gentleman" [5] is attached and who is charmed by the music quality of an orderly kitchen, is surely not a wit. What is especially important is that there be some empty space between the various kinds of stored implements: even that empty space affords as beautiful and as pure a sight as the void in the midst of a dithyrambic chorus. Ischomachos

[5] VI.14.

clinches his argument by contrasting the ease with which a servant [6] finds the things he is sent to buy on the market, with the difficulty one frequently has in finding a human being; the reason is that in the first case there exists a fixed place and in the second case there is none. One must wonder whether Ischomachos' failing to meet the strangers for whom he is waiting in the colonnade of Zeus the Deliverer,[7] is due to the strangers' carelessness.

[6] Cf. *Cyrop.* VIII.5.13, where Xenophon, speaking in his own name but expressing his Cyrus' thought, speaks of sensible or sober servants: is Ischomachos more sanguine than Xenophon?

[7] VII.2, XII.1–2.

Gynaikologia—III: Order, II
(Chapter IX)

The particularly close connection between this chapter and
the preceding one appears immediately from their contents. In
addition, it is indicated by the close resemblance between the
beginnings of the two chapters. Both chapters open with a
question of Socrates concerning the effect of Ischomachos'
teaching on his wife. At the beginning of the preceding chapter he had asked him whether his wife was stirred by his conversing with her to greater care: the care as such antedated the
lecture. Now Socrates asks him whether his wife seemed to
him to listen in any way to what he had so earnestly tried to
teach her. Ischomachos replies (without swearing) that she
promised to take care, that she was visibly very glad to have
been freed from her embarrassment, and that she asked that he
should as soon as possible bring their things in order in the
manner stated by him: her concern with order did not ante-
date the lecture. Thereupon Socrates asks him how he brought
their things in order for her. The question concerns no longer
the goodness, the easiness, and the beauty of order, but the
order itself.

Ischomachos began with setting forth to his wife the apti-
tude of his house, or rather of each of its rooms, for being the
most convenient receptacle for whatever was to be put into it;
the rooms had been designed for this very purpose. His teaching on the house agrees to some extent with that of Socrates,
which is based on the explicit identification of the beautiful
with the good or useful. The most striking difference between

the two teachings is that Socrates explicitly demands, and Ischomachos does not, that the house be most pleasant to live
in.[1] After having shown to his wife that the whole house is
built sensibly, he draws her attention in particular to the fact
that the women's quarters are separated by a bolted door from
the men's quarters so that the master and the mistress can control the generation of children by the servants. Then the
spouses set about separating one from another according to
tribes, their things to be ordered. They began by collecting
the things they would use in sacrificing. Thereafter they separated the woman's ornaments for festivals, the man's clothing
for festivals and war, bedding for the women's quarters, bedding for the men's quarters, shoes for women, shoes for men.
We note that the implements for women are mentioned before
the implements for men; this underlines the fact that in the
Oeconomicus the *gynaikologia* precedes the *andrologia*. Another tribe consisted of armor, another of tools for spinning,
another of tools for breadmaking, another of tools for cooking, another of the things used for bathing, another of the
things used for kneading bread, another of the things used at
the table. The things belonging to the seven,[2] or twice seven,
tribes they divided into those for everyday use and those for
use at feasts. After having separated all these things according
to tribes, they carried each sort to its proper place.

Ischomachos' separating his indoor things according to tribes
in order to establish order within his house reminds us of Socrates' separating the beings according to races or kinds in order
to discover the order of the whole. According to Xenophon,
Socrates "never ceased considering with his companions what
each of the beings is," i.e., what each kind of the beings is. He

[1] *Mem.* III.8.8–10. Cf. above, p. 121.
[2] Cf. *Symp.* 4.45; *Iliad* IX.122–23; *Mem.* III.7.6 and III.4.7.

called this activity or art "dialectics," which means literally the art of conversation. He asserted that the activity is called *dialegesthai* with a view to the fact that men coming together for joint deliberation pick or select (*dialegein*) things according to races or kinds.[3] We are forced to wonder whether Ischomachos' separating his indoor things according to tribes is not the model for the peculiarly Socratic philosophizing. We recall that Socrates approached Ischomachos in order to learn from him what perfect gentlemanship is. We recall further that the example par excellence of order was meant to educate, not only Ischomachos' wife, but even Socrates. The question regarding the perfect gentleman may be said to comprise all the questions regarding human things which Socrates was always raising, like What is pious? What is impious? What is noble? What is base? and so on;[4] these questions call for separating, for instance, what is pious from what is noble. It seems then that Ischomachos was in a manner the source, not only of Socrates' substantive knowledge of the human things, but also of his way of acquiring that knowledge, of his "method." That a model economist should have played such a role in Socrates' life is not as surprising, or even absurd, as it may well seem at first hearing. For Socrates' most comprehensive teaching, his teaching which transcends the human things, deals with the order of the whole cosmos, the order that serves the benefit of men and is due to the god's *oikonomein*.[5] It is true that the teleotheology is exposed to difficulties. In the *Memorabilia*, Socrates says that the divine has no needs;[6] can there be "economy" if there are no needs? Above all, it is not clear how

---

[3] *Mem.* IV.5.12, IV.6.1. Ischomachos speaks of *dialegein* in *Oec.* VIII.9.
[4] *Mem.* I.1.16, IV.6.13–15.
[5] *Mem.* IV.3.13, I.4.8, I.4.13, and contexts.
[6] *Mem.* I.6.10; cf. I.4.10.

Socrates' theology is connected with the "What is . . ." questions which he never ceased raising. In the *Oeconomicus*, Ischomachos indicates some doubts regarding the teleotheology. In particular, in the section devoted to "order" there is almost complete silence about the god or the gods, and we find there even less support for the teleotheology than before. As for Socrates, he speaks in the *Oeconomicus* of the gods as at least as much disturbers of the philanthropic order as its supporters; he is silent during Ischomachos' lectures on order; later on he says that the gods do not rule the year in an ordered manner.[7] One is therefore tempted to wonder whether the Xenophontic Socrates was not, like the Platonic Socrates, dissatisfied with the simple teleology—anthropocentric or not—which at first glance seems to supply the most rational solution to all difficulties, and turned for this reason to the "What is . . ." questions or to "the separating of beings according to kinds." [8]

The suggestion that Ischomachos was in a manner the source of both Socrates' substantive knowledge of the human things and of his "method" is a deliberate exaggeration that is meant to counteract the amazing neglect of the *Oeconomicus* on the part of those who are concerned with "the Socratic problem." Every child can see the difference between the rather pedantic husband's teaching his wife how to establish an order according to tribes among her pots and pans, or at any rate among artifacts, and Socrates' attempting to discover the order of the whole by distinguishing the kinds of beings that make up the whole and by finding out what each of those kinds is. For, as

[7] XVII.4.

[8] *Phaedo* 97c3–98b6, 99c6–e6. Cf. the parallel development on a higher level—the level of the "kinds" or "ideas"—and in this sense at a later stage, as reported in the *Parmenides* 130b7–e4. The "What is . . ." questions are meant to dispose of the questions regarding the "material and efficient causes" of the natural species.

Xenophon intimates by saying that Socrates never ceased considering what each of the beings is, Socrates did not limit his inquiry to the human things. Someone might say that "beings" means here "the things that are good and noble," but this identification is made by Virtue herself or rather by the sophist Prodikos.[9] That Socrates was not merely concerned with human things is shown sufficiently by his teleotheology, however precarious that teaching might be. Socrates blamed indeed the men who worried about the nature of all things as madmen, but for what reason? To some of them it seems that being is one, to others that there are infinitely many beings; to some of them it seems that all things are always in motion, to others that nothing is ever moved; to some of them it seems that everything comes into being and perishes, to others that nothing ever comes into being or perishes.[10] That is to say, according to the view which is sane and sober, there are only a finite number of beings (which makes sense only if it is not said of individual beings), and there are some beings which never change and which never come into being or perish, namely, the kinds. This is not to deny that Socrates apparently limited his "What is . . ." questions to "the human things" as distinguished from all beings strictly understood; but this appearance is ultimately of importance only because it points to the humble ("Ischomachean") origin of the philosophizing peculiar to him.

After Ischomachos and his wife had separated their utensils from one another according to tribes, they brought them to their appropriate places and then showed the servants who had to use them every day where they are kept, and entrusted them to their care; the rest of the utensils they handed over to

[9] *Mem.* II.1.27–28.
[10] *Mem.* I.1.13–14.

the housekeeper with the necessary instructions, after having counted them and made a written list of them. They had appointed as housekeeper a woman who seemed to be most temperate regarding the various kinds of bodily pleasures, to have a good memory, and, as regards the future, to be very eager to avoid punishment for negligence and to earn respect by gratifying her master and mistress. They also taught her by the proper means to be well-meaning toward them and to become concerned in helping them to increase their estate. Last but not least, they put justice into her. It should be noted that Ischomachos does not say anything about his educating his wife in continence and in justice, and still less about his having succeeded in it. One cannot explain this silence by suggesting that she was already sufficiently educated in these respects when he married her, for, as he told Socrates earlier, she had not received any education to speak of prior to her marriage, or, as Socrates himself occasionally indicated, the sons are the children to be educated, while the daughters are to be watched.[11] Ischomachos did teach his wife that in cities subject to good laws the citizens elect guardians of the law who see to it that the laws are observed; she must regard herself as the guardian of the laws laid down by them for the house; she must inspect the utensils as the commander of a garrison inspects the guards; like a queen, she must reward and punish everyone according to his deserts. He taught her in addition that she had no right to complain if he imposed on her a heavier burden regarding their possessions than on the servants, since the possessions belong to the master and not to the servants: to him who derives the greatest benefit from the preservation of the possessions and the greatest harm from their destruction, it most properly belongs to exercise the greatest care in regard to

[11] VII.4–6; cf. *Mem.* I.5.2.

them. At this point Socrates, who had been as silent throughout the bulk of the chapter as the wife had been during the lecture, asked Ischomachos whether his wife was in any way disposed to heed what she had heard from him. His wife replied, he replied, that he was wrong if he believed that he imposed on her a heavy burden by teaching her how to take care of their things; it would be harder on her if he had commanded her to neglect her things, for just as it is natural, as it seems, for a sensible or sober woman to take care of her children rather than to neglect them, so, she held, it is more pleasant for such a woman to take care of her possessions, which are gratifying by the mere fact that they are her own, than to neglect them. In the chapters on order it is only Ischomachos' wife who ever speaks of nature or the natural; she never speaks of order. Her husband, the teacher of order, on the other hand, speaks of law. In the same chapters gods are mentioned only in the utterance, reported by Ischomachos, of the Phoenician sailor; not a single oath occurs in the discussion of order.

Gynaikologia—IV: Cosmetics
(Chapter X)

The chapter that follows the section on order is as dialogic as the chapter preceding that section. Both Socrates and Ischomachos' wife are now again presented as speaking to Ischomachos to a greater degree than in the section on order. Socrates expresses to Ischomachos his admiration, not for Ischomachos' lectures on order, but for his wife's masculine mind as shown by her reply to her husband; in so doing, he swears, "By Hera." In his report to Kritoboulos and the other friends, he underlines the fact that he uses a woman's oath, that he behaves like a woman, in contrast to the masculine character of Ischomachos' wife, whose reply revealed that virile concern with one's own which makes human beings good defenders of their own. We recall again that manliness is not mentioned by Xenophon among Socrates' virtues. Ischomachos is understandably willing to give Socrates other examples of his wife's high-mindedness, i.e., of her obeying him quickly after having heard his suggestions only once. For other reasons Socrates is no less willing to learn about things of this kind: it is much more pleasant for him to learn of the virtue of a living woman than if Zeuxis showed him the portrait of a beautiful woman whom he had painted. He had given no such sign of eagerness to learn in the section on order. The beautiful woman whom Zeuxis shows after having painted her is of course also a living woman. To preserve the full force of Socrates' antithesis, it seems therefore preferable to understand him as meaning that he prefers to learn of the virtue of a living woman rather than to look, under Zeuxis' guidance, at a portrait made by him of a beautiful woman. In that case, however, he is likely to be as much interested in Zeuxis' reproduction as in the original. But is the same not true of his learning of the virtue of the living woman? For he learns of that virtue not through seeing Ischomachos' wife but through a report about her: he looks at the virtue of Ischomachos' wife with the eyes of Ischomachos, just as he would look at a beautiful woman portrayed by Zeuxis with the eyes of Zeuxis. The irregularity of Socrates' expression draws our attention to the facts that Socrates is at least as much interested in Ischomachos' report about his wife's virtue as in that virtue itself and that he has no first-hand knowledge of her virtue. Socrates prefers to hear Ischomachos' report about his wife's virtue rather than to see a beautiful woman portrayed by the best painter, although Ischomachos is not likely to be as good an interpreter of his wife's virtue as Zeuxis is of the beauty of a woman whom he has portrayed. This is not to deny that Socrates' statement can easily induce one to think that the beauty of a living human being can be surpassed by a painter's imitation, while the virtue of a living human being cannot be surpassed or even rivaled by a poet's or a writer's imitation. We surely do not go wrong if we assert that Xenophon regarded his reproduction of Socrates' virtue for more than one reason as inferior to that virtue itself, one reason being that in publicly presenting Socrates' virtue he could not assume that he was speaking only to friends.[1]

Socrates' reference to Zeuxis, who in a manner beautifies the beautiful, proves to be a divination of what Ischomachos is about to tell. Once upon a time he saw that his wife had used artificial means to improve on her being, the truth, or her nature. She had acted, that is, as Vice herself acted, according to

[1] Cf. *Mem.* IV.7.1 with *Oec.* VI.13–15.

Socrates' rendering of Prodikos' story, when she tried to se-
duce Herakles at the crossroads, or as the first Cyrus acted, according to Xenophon, in order to beguile his subjects.[2] The
perfect gentleman Ischomachos has no use for such practices.
He asked his wife whether she would judge him more worthy
to be beloved as a partner in their wealth if he disclosed to her
their things just as they are without boasting or concealment,
or if he tried to deceive her by pretending to be richer than he
is, and in particular by showing her counterfeit money and
other shams as if they were genuine. His wife broke in
"straightway," "at once." This is the only occasion on which
she or her husband says something "straightway": Ischomachos is sedate, and his wife is shy. But now she becomes lively,
since she must repel the thought that her husband might deceive her about his property by boasting or by concealment;
she thus shows again how masculine her mind is in regard to
her own. She is shocked by Ischomachos' question; she could
not love him from her heart, from her soul, if he were a man
who would do such things. Thereupon he applies what they
had agreed upon regarding their sharing of their property to
their sharing of one another's body. He asks her first whether
they had not come together also in order to share each other's
bodies; his modest wife replies that this is at any rate what
people say. He asks her then whether she would not prefer to
sense his body itself rather than shams which, at any rate,
would not survive an embrace. She replies that to sense his
body itself is more pleasant to her than to sense the artifacts in
question. He clinches the issue by telling her that he feels the
same: just as the gods have made horses most pleasant to
horses, cattle most pleasant to cattle, and sheep most pleasant
to sheep, so human beings regard the genuine body of a human

[2] *Mem.* II.1.22; *Cyrop.* VIII.1.40–41, VIII.2.26, VIII.3.14.

being most pleasant. The lack of parallelism is justified by the fact that nature enables human beings, as distinguished from the brutes, to invent and use cosmetics. After having shown in the section on order that men can and to some extent even must improve on nature, Ischomachos now calls his wife back from an unnecessary and undesirable deviation from nature, from a deviation which originates in the wish to deceive. In other words, after having devoted the section on order to genuine beauty, he speaks in the subsequent chapter of spurious beauty.

The firm stand taken by Ischomachos for nature, or truth, against deception induces Socrates, not to approve of that stand or indeed to question it, but to ask him how his wife replied to what he had said. He learns that she replied by deed and by speech. She never again used cosmetics but tried to present herself undisguised and in a becoming manner. She asked her husband whether he could not advise her how she could come to sight as beautiful in truth and not merely in appearance. He advised her not always to sit about like a slave woman or a pretentious lady but to do her work as mistress of the house and to take exercise by doing the kind of housework that befits her; by acting thus, the wife will look more attractive to her husband than her maid, to whom she will be superior anyway by her superior cleanliness and dress and by the voluntary character of her submission. Ischomachos concludes by assuring Socrates that his wife still behaves now as he had taught her then and as he tells Socrates now.

This is the end of the *gynaikologia*. Ischomachos might have continued his account of how he had educated his wife if Socrates had not put a stop to it by saying that he had heard enough about the deeds of his wife "for the present." The expression implies that the *gynaikologia* is not complete. If it were complete, Socrates' promise to Kritoboulos to bring him together with Aspasia would have been out of place. Besides, the *gynaikologia* is incomplete for another reason. Some time has elapsed between Ischomachos' conversation with Socrates, and still more between Socrates' report of that conversation to Kritoboulos, and Ischomachos' original conversation with his wife. It would be of some interest to know how profound and lasting the impression was which Ischomachos' admonitions had made on his wife. The *Oeconomicus* is as silent about this subject as it is about the success of Socrates' teaching Kritoboulos the rudiments of household management. We do not know with which Ischomachos Socrates conversed about perfect gentlemanship, and hence which Ischomachos' wife was presented by her husband as the model of a wife. Let us have a look at Xenophon's two other minor Socratic writings. The *Symposion* is located in the house of Kallias, the son of Hipponikos. The *Apology of Socrates* is primarily a conversation between Socrates and Hermogenes, the brother of Kallias.[3] There was an Ischomachos who was a father-in-law of Kallias, and that Ischomachos had a quite remarkable wife. As we learn from a contemporary orator,[4] Kallias married a daughter of Ischomachos, but he had not been living with her a year before he made her mother his mistress, and he lived with mother and daughter together, while being the priest of Mother and Daughter, i.e., of Demeter and Kore,[5] and kept them both in his house together. Ischomachos' daughter thought death preferable to living with such things before her eyes; but her attempt to hang herself failed; after she recovered, she ran away from her house: the mother had expelled the daughter. But

[3] Cf. Plato, *Cratylus* 391b11–c3.
[4] Andocides, *On the Mysteries* 124–27.
[5] Hence Kallias is a kind of Pluto-Hades; cf. the implication of Plato, *Protagoras* 315b9, and 315c8.

Kallias tired of the mother as well and expelled her in turn. She then said that she was pregnant by him, but when she gave birth to a son, Kallias denied his paternity. Years afterward Kallias fell in love with that most impudent hag and received her again into his house and said that the boy was his son. It is impossible to assert that Xenophon's Ischomachos was Kallias' father-in-law or even that Xenophon knew of that scandalous story. But one can safely say that what Xenophon's Socrates reports about Ischomachos and his wife is perfectly compatible with the possibility that that woman proved in later years to be less good than her pedagogic husband expected her to become and that this disappointing truth was known to Socrates and his friends when he gave them his report. If Socrates failed to educate Xanthippe,[6] he was superior to Ischomachos by having no delusions in this respect or by being aware of his ignorance of the art of managing one's wife.

[6] Cf. *Symp.* 2.10.

𝄐𝄐𝄐𝄐𝄐 *Andrologia* (Chapter XI)

Socrates puts a stop to Ischomachos' report about his wife's doings by asking him to tell him of his own doings; i.e., he turns now to the subject for the sake of whose understanding he had approached Ischomachos in the first place. He eases the burden that he imposes on Ischomachos through his request by saying that Ischomachos will be pleased to speak of the things to which he owes his high reputation and that Socrates will be very grateful to him after hearing a full account of the doings of the perfect gentleman and after, if he can do so, understanding it. In contradistinction to Kritoboulos,[1] Socrates does not express the wish to become a perfect gentleman himself. Ischomachos is glad to comply with Socrates' request for the additional reason that Socrates might set him right if in any point he does not seem to him to act well. Socrates finds fault with that reason: a man who is the model of a perfect gentleman cannot in justice be corrected by a man who is reputed to be an idle talker and to measure the air, and who is reproached on account of his poverty. He thus begins to make clear the profound difference between himself and the perfect gentleman: Socrates is not a perfect gentleman. A perfect gentleman will never engage in activities which would bring him the reputation of being an idle talker and of measuring the air—a reputation which Socrates acquired at least partly through Aristophanes[2] and other comic poets. Above all, a perfect gentleman must be wealthy in the ordinary meaning of the

---

[1] VI.12.
[2] *Clouds* 225, 1480, 1485; cf. *Birds* 995.

term. Socrates says of the reproach made to him on account of his poverty that it seems (is thought) to be most foolish. He explains his assertion by narrating an experience which he had had. He would have been greatly depressed by the charge of being poor if he had not lately seen the horse of Nikias the foreigner, which was followed by many men who looked at it with admiration, some of whom praised it highly. Socrates approached the groom with the question whether the horse had much money. The groom looked at him as if he were not only grossly ignorant but not even sane, and said: How can a horse have any money? When he had heard this, Socrates recovered from his depression, for he realized that if a horse, although penniless, can become good, provided it has a soul by nature good, Socrates could become a good man. The reproach on account of poverty is then palpably foolish, since if it made sense, a horse would need money in order to be good. Socrates' inference is based on the tacit premise that he possesses a soul by nature good, i.e., that he can learn quickly, remember what he has learned, and long for all branches of knowledge through which one can nobly dwell in a house and a city and altogether make a good use of human beings and of human affairs.[3] The story is as characteristic of Socrates as the stories of Cyrus and of the Phoenician boatswain are of Lysander and Ischomachos respectively. Socrates has not met with barbarians; he is as remote from barbarians, from barbarism, as possible; on the other hand, he acquires his most important insight into the character of true human virtue by considering the virtue of a horse: true human virtue is not in need of conventions. Since he is then satisfied that he can become a good man, he asks Ischomachos to give him a full account of what he does, so as to enable him, to the extent to which he can under-

[3] *Mem.* IV.1.2.

stand it by listening, to imitate him, not indeed straightway but starting tomorrow. One is tempted to say that Socrates has his conversation with Ischomachos on the day after he had learned indirectly through Nikias' groom that he could acquire virtue, and on the day before he began to acquire it; surely that conversation made an epoch in his life.

Yet even Ischomachos is aware that Socrates is joking. But the joke points to the serious difference between Ischomachos' virtue or gentlemanship, which Socrates lacks—and whose lack he does not even deplore—and Socrates' virtue or gentleman-ship, which both antedated and survived his conversation with Ischomachos. The most massive difference between the two kinds of virtue is that the former presupposes and the latter does not presuppose the possession of considerable wealth. Seen in the light of this difference, the virtue of the economist Ischomachos, of the freeman who is a member of a republic, a commonwealth, and who minds his own business, and the vir-tue of the king Cyrus, the sole and absolute ruler of an im-mense empire, whose own business is completely absorbed into his concern for millions of men, are fundamentally the same. Hence, Cyrus or Ischomachos on the one hand and Socrates on the other stand at opposite poles of Xenophon's "moral uni-verse." The difference to which Xenophon points is the same as that of which Aristotle speaks as that between the practical, or political, and the theoretical life; the former needs "external equipment" to a much greater degree than the latter.[4] The dif-ference to which Xenophon points is the same as that which Plato articulates as that between political, or vulgar, and genu-ine virtue.[5]

Ischomachos' full account of his activity begins with his

[4] *Eth. Nic.* 1178a23–b5.
[5] *Phaedo* 82a18–c1; cf. *Laws* 710a.

serving the gods. He "seems" to have realized that while the gods do not permit men to become happy unless they are prudent and do assiduously what prudence prescribes, prudence and assiduity are not the sufficient condition of human happiness; the gods may refuse success to men however prudent and diligent. Ischomachos acts then on the view stated by the Phoenician boatswain; but he states that view in a somewhat less shocking or savage manner than the Phoenician. The happiness at which he aims consists of these parts: health, strength of the body, honor in the city, good will on the part of his friends, and in war safety with honor and honorable increase of wealth.[6] This enumeration shows why there is no radical separation of the economic, or private, and the political life.[7]

Socrates, who is poor and satisfied with being poor, is apparently struck most by Ischomachos' concern with being wealthy and his willingness to undergo the many troubles which accompany the possession of wealth. But Ischomachos sees only pleasure where Socrates sees only trouble; wealth is pleasant because it enables a man to honor the gods magnificently, to assist his friends in their need, and to contribute toward the adornment of the city. These purposes for which wealth is to be used and which justify the concern with the acquisition of wealth are not selfish; this is perhaps sufficient reason for Socrates to call them, not indeed pleasant, but noble; to this extent the pupil Socrates has become convinced by Ischomachos' defense of the perfect gentleman's way of life. Ischomachos' statement further implies, as Socrates explains, that the perfect gentleman must be concerned not only, like the general run of men, with managing the household but with increasing it; such increase is required because of his de-

---

[6] Cf. the list of the parts of happiness in Aristotle's *Rhetoric* I.5.
[7] Cf. II.5 with *Mem.* II.1.8 ff. (especially 13–14).

sire to adorn the city and to support his friends. It seems that honoring the gods magnificently is understood by Socrates as part of adorning the city.[8] He certainly makes it clear that he belongs to the many who are able to praise the perfect gentlemen's pursuit and use of wealth but unable to imitate them. He turns therefore for the time being to Ischomachos' pursuit of those three ends which can be pursued also by men like himself: health, strength of the body, and honorable escape even from war. Ischomachos is doubtful whether the separation, proposed by Socrates, of the pursuit of these three ends from the pursuit of increase of wealth is feasible. Socrates agrees: he surely is eager to hear the full account of how the perfect gentleman spends the day.

We mention only a few points. He rises early and spends as much time as he can in the open air, walking, running, or riding on horseback. When he has no business in town, he takes a close look at what his field hands are doing. Thereafter as a rule he jumps on his horse and goes through equestrian exercises that resemble as nearly as possible those needed in war. After this is over, his servant "gives the horse a roll and leads it home." In Aristophanes' *Clouds*, Pheidippides says to his servant in his dream—even in his dream: "Give the horse a roll and lead it home." [9] Ischomachos, we shall say, is Xenophon's substitute for the Aristophanean Pheidippides. The Aristophanean Socrates corrupted completely a youth who was already half-corrupted by horsemanship and who was the son of a farmer; the Xenophontic Socrates leads a young man who is the son of a gentleman-farmer, and who is in danger of losing

[8] "Aristoteli ut veteribus omnibus extra Ecclesiam cultus deorum sub magnificentia ponitur" (Jakob Gronovius' note on Hugo Grotius' *De jure belli ac pacis*, Prolegomena, sect. 45).

[9] *Clouds* 32.

himself in frivolities, back to farming or saves him from corruption by teaching him, among other things, the rudiments of
farming. In contradistinction to the Aristophanean Socrates,
who is nothing but a teacher, the Xenophontic Socrates is in
the first place a pupil, not of idle talkers, i.e., of alien sophists
or students of nature, but of the most perfect gentleman in
Athens. That perfect gentleman teaches him, without knowing
it, the rudiments of the right kind of philosophizing. Whereas
the pupil of the Aristophanean Socrates looked down on his
farming father, the teacher of the Xenophontic Socrates ad-
mires his farming father.[10] The *Oeconomicus* is then in a
properly subdued manner a comical reply to Aristophanes'
comical attack on Socrates. More precisely, the *Oeconomicus*
describes Socrates' famous turning away from his earlier pursuit, which brought him the reputation of being an idle talker
and a man who measures the air and which left him wholly
unaware of what perfect gentlemanship is, toward the study of
only the human things and the things useful to human beings.
This profound change that took place after the comical attacks
on Socrates seems to be traced in Plato's *Apology of Socrates*
to the Delphic god [11] or to Chairephon, the companion par
excellence of Socrates in the *Clouds;* it was traced by Xenophon, it seems, to the comic poet himself—to a man who,
through his comedies, kept Kritoboulos away from farming,
from performing his filial duties. Both Plato and Xenophon
treat Socrates' "pre-Socratic" past with great delicacy. Plato
makes his master tell the story of that past—a story which
partly confirms the account given in the *Clouds*—to his friends
when he was already beyond the reach of those who condemn
the study of nature as wicked. The Ischomachos section of the

[10] XX.22–28.
[11] Xenophon, *Apol. Socr.* 14.

Oeconomicus is at any rate a worthy part of *the* Socratic discourse written by Xenophon.

Swearing again by Hera, Socrates expresses his admiration for Ischomachos' taking care successfully at the same time of his health, his strength, his fitness for war, and his wealth; his success, partly due to the gods, in regard to health and strength is visible, while his success in regard to horsemanship and wealth is the talk of the town. Ischomachos replies that these great successes lead, not so much to his being called by many a perfect gentleman, as to his being slandered very much by many. Even at the time of his conversation with Ischomachos, Socrates already knows enough of the ways of the world not to be surprised by Ischomachos' fate, but Ischomachos' reply affords him an easy transition to a further question, the answer to which completes the account of the perfect gentleman or the confrontation of the two incompatible ways of life. He asks Ischomachos whether he takes care to be skilled also in debate—in giving accounts to others and demanding them from others. Ischomachos replies by asking whether he does not seem to Socrates to practice constantly this very thing, i.e., defending himself by not doing wrong to anyone and by doing good as much as he can to many, and accusing others by watching those who privately wrong many and who wrong the city and do no good to anyone. This reply reminds us of the reply that Socrates gave when he was blamed for not thinking about his defense against the charge made by Meletos: "Do I not seem to you to have spent my whole life preparing that defense? For did I do anything but consider thoroughly the just and unjust things and do the just things while abstaining from the unjust ones?" [12] Ischomachos did not, like Socrates, spend his life considering the just and unjust things—

[12] *Mem.* IV.8.4. Cf. *Apol. Socr.* 3.

this would be "idle talk." Socrates, on the other hand, was not in any way concerned with accusing others.[13] Socrates is not satisfied with Ischomachos' reply, because it says nothing as to whether he is concerned with putting into words what in his view is conducive to his defense and to the accusation of others. Ischomachos assures him that he never ceases to practice speaking, and by no means only defending himself and accusing others; he practices all kinds of speaking: forensic, praising as well as blaming, and deliberative. He adds the remark that he was frequently condemned, not indeed by any court of law, but by his wife; for he cannot plead his cause well if it is useful to him to say the untruth; swearing by Zeus, he says that he cannot make the weaker argument the stronger one. Socrates, who—in contradistinction to Ischomachos—could do what he liked with anyone disputing with him,[14] corrects him by saying: "Perhaps you cannot make the untruth true." The Socrates who conversed with Ischomachos was as much a rhetorician as Aristophanes' Socrates. Someone might say that Socrates is not likely to have fared better in his arguments with Xanthippe than Ischomachos in his arguments with his wife. But if we may generalize from the only pertinent example given to us by Xenophon,[15] Socrates did not even begin to argue with Xanthippe: when his son Lamprokles complained about his mother's unbearable conduct toward him, Socrates did not take up the matter with his wife but persuaded his son to change his conduct, i.e., to change his reaction to his mother's unchangeable conduct.

[13] Cf. *Gorgias* 480b7–481b1.
[14] *Mem.* I.2.14. Cf. *Kynegetikos* 3.9.
[15] *Mem.* II.2.

How to educate stewards to good will and diligence (Chapter XII)

Socrates seems to have learned everything about perfect gentlemanship that he wished to learn. At any rate, he apprehends now that he might be detaining Ischomachos. Ischomachos reassures him: he does not wish to leave now, and by his staying his affairs will not be neglected, for he keeps stewards on his farms. As Socrates finds out at once, Ischomachos educates his stewards; hence the account of the stewards is an account of Ischomachos' educating his stewards, just as the account of the wife was an account of Ischomachos' educating his wife. The perfect gentleman is an educator. Here is an important link between the perfect gentleman and Socrates: Socrates regarded himself later as an expert on education and only on education.[1] This is not to assert that he was an expert on the education of wives and stewards. Ischomachos educates his stewards himself, since they have to take his place in his absence as regards the work on the farms and therefore must know no more and no less than he knows about that work. Socrates infers that the stewards must possess benevolence or good will toward their master and what belongs to him. Such good will is indeed the first thing to which Ischomachos tries to educate his stewards. Socrates seems to be surprised by Ischomachos' implicit claim that he can instill good will toward himself and what belongs to him in anyone he wishes. For Ischomachos, however, this is the easiest thing in the world: one makes people benevolent toward oneself by benefiting them

1 *Apol. Socr.* 20–21; cf. Plato, *Laches* 180b7–d3.

from what one has in abundance. The Socrates who was notorious only as an idle talker and as a measurer of the air is not as sanguine or as simple-minded as Ischomachos,[2] but he does not see fit to deprive Ischomachos of his simplicity: Ischomachos is not likely to remain, or to have become, as wealthy as he is if he does not possess within himself a corrective to that simplicity. He merely reminds him of the limitations of good will: all sane men have good will toward themselves, and yet not all men are willing to undergo the trouble without which one cannot acquire the good things one likes to have. Ischomachos replies that he also teaches his stewards seriously to care for his property or to be diligent in their work. This claim surprises Socrates still more than Ischomachos' preceding claim: hitherto he believed that diligence was not teachable at all. If we assume that diligence is a virtue or at least an indispensable ingredient of every virtue, then Socrates did not believe, at least at the time at which he conversed with Ischomachos, that virtue is teachable. Ischomachos grants to Socrates that not all men can be taught to be diligent, and therewith that not all men can be taught to be virtuous. Socrates is very eager to know which kind of man is teachable in this respect. It is easier for Ischomachos—although even this is not quite easy for him—to tell Socrates what kinds of men cannot be taught to be diligent. Those kinds are those who are incontinent with regard to wine, those who are incontinent with regard to sleep, and those who are passionately in love. But Socrates wishes to know what desire animates those who are educable. It seems that Ischomachos, if left to himself, would have been unable to satisfy Socrates, or in other words, that prior to his conversation with Ischomachos, Socrates already possessed a better un-

[2] Cf. *Symp.* 3.4 and 4.1–3.

derstanding of education than did the perfect gentleman. Socrates asks him whether those who are passionately in love with lucre are also not educable to diligence in farm work. Ischomachos replies that they are excellently disposed to such diligence; they merely have to be shown that that diligence is lucrative to them. Socrates suggests a qualification: the potential stewards' love of lucre must not be extreme. Besides, it appears that the profit which Ischomachos' stewards can expect if they are diligent consists of Ischomachos' praising them and his attempting to honor them, or in their avoiding verbal and other hurt that their master might inflict on them. Finally, Socrates turns from the men to be educated to the educator: Must not the teacher of diligence be himself diligent? Socrates speaks of the teacher of diligence in general; he does not raise the question as to whether a man like himself, who is not a diligent farmer, can make someone like Kritoboulos a diligent farmer. The whole *Oeconomicus* seems to be based on the assumption that the teaching of a diligent farmer can be successfully transmitted by a nonfarmer to a potential farmer. It is doubtful whether diligence can be thus conveyed from Ischomachos to Kritoboulos. According to Ischomachos, a careless man can as little make other men careful as an unmusic man can make other men music. On the other hand, the diligence of the master is only the necessary condition of the diligence of the servants; a diligent master may have careless servants despite the fact that they will be deservedly punished. On the whole that barbarian was right who replied to the Persian king that it is the master's eye that fattens a horse most quickly. Teaching not accompanied by coercion or, more precisely, by despotic power is insufficient for the education of stewards.

When Ischomachos speaks of the various kinds of continence that are required of the stewards, he does not mention continence of the belly—a kind of continence he had mentioned when speaking of what is required of the housekeeper.[3] Perhaps Xenophon merely indicates by this that something of importance is consciously omitted by him but unconsciously omitted by Ischomachos. It goes without saying that when referring to the master's eye, Ischomachos thinks only of the eye of the mortal master. While the chapter under discussion has a greater density of oaths than any other chapter of the work, it is completely silent on piety as an objective or ingredient of the education of the stewards.[4] Nor is piety demanded as such an objective or ingredient in the two other chapters devoted to the education of stewards. Nor is a word said to the effect that that education belongs to the works which must be begun piously.[5] The powerful presence of the human master makes the recourse to divine masters less necessary than it otherwise would be.

It seems that the diligent steward is not necessarily filled with good will toward his master or that the good steward needs some good will toward his master in addition to his diligence.[6]

[3] IX.11; cf. *Mem.* I.5.1 and II.6.1.
[4] Cf. Leo Strauss, *On Tyranny* (Ithaca, N.Y.: Cornell University Press, 1968), pp. 68 and 71.
[5] Cf. V.19–VI.1 and VII.7–8. *On Tyranny*, pp. 127–128.
[6] Cf. XV.1 and XV.5.

⌘⌘⌘⌘⌘ How to educate stewards to rulership (Chapter XIII)

Socrates learns from Ischomachos that in addition to being diligent, the steward must know what is to be done on the farm as well as how to do it, and that he must have learned to rule the field hands. Ischomachos modestly claims that he tries to educate his stewards to rulership (or ability to rule). Even this modest claim astonishes Socrates, who has no notion of how Ischomachos educates human beings to rulership. Ischomachos does not think that his way of achieving this result is grand; on the contrary, he thinks that if Socrates hears of it, he may find it laughable. Socrates protests strongly against Ischomachos' judgment and apprehension; on no other occasion in the discussion of stewardship does he oppose so strongly his knowledge to Ischomachos' opinion as when the rank of rulership, and hence of education to rulership, is the theme: whoever can make men capable of ruling over human beings can obviously teach them how to be masters of human beings, and whoever can teach men to be masterly can teach them to be kingly. In other words, there is no essential difference between the rule exercised by a steward over the field hands and the rule exercised by the kingly man.[1] Ischomachos does not protest against this contention which fits in so well with the praise of his ability to educate his stewards to rulership.[2]

[1] Cf. *Mem.* III.4.12 and Plato, *Statesman* 258e8–259c5.
[2] Cf. VII.3, beginning.

While Socrates knows everything about the high rank of education to rulership, he apparently knows nothing about how that education is achieved; he surely listens in silence to Ischomachos' exposition of this subject.

A man able to rule is a man able to make other beings obey. The other animals, strong or weak, learn to obey men by being punished for trying to disobey and by being well treated for eagerly doing what men want them to do. Human beings can be induced to obey by speech, i.e., if one explains to them that it is useful to them to obey. But as regards slaves also the education held to be fit only for beasts is very helpful, for they can be induced to obey if one gratifies their bellies. The ambitious natures among them, on the other hand, are spurred on by praise, for some natures are as hungry for praise as others are for food and drink. By the means mentioned, Ischomachos makes his workers obey him and expects his stewards to make the hands obey them. In addition to influencing his workers through their bellies and their desire for praise, Ischomachos spurs them on by honoring the better ones among them with better clothes and shoes and by giving inferior things to the inferior men.

Ischomachos speaks chiefly of how he makes his workers obey either him directly or his stewards. But it is clear that his education of his stewards toward obedience to him does not differ from his education of the better sort of his workers. The education must induce the workers not only to toil but also to expose themselves to dangers, and this is true a fortiori of the stewards; to that extent Ischomachos is also a teacher of courage or manliness, although he never uses this term. Since in the case of the workers, at any rate, he appeals to their bellies, he would not achieve his goal if they were too continent in this respect. Perhaps this explains his silence in the preced-

ing chapter on continence regarding the belly; the line between what is required of the workers and what is required of
the stewards is not drawn too clearly; after all, both kinds of
men are slaves.

⚄⚄⚄⚄⚄ How to educate stewards to justice (Chapter XIV)

Socrates learns from Ischomachos that in addition to being capable of ruling, the steward must abstain from his master's property. Ischomachos, who does not take any chances, explains to Socrates why a thieving steward is ruinous. It seems that honesty does not necessarily flow from benevolence,[1] for however benevolent a man may be to another man, he is more benevolent to himself.[2] Socrates does not wonder about the fact that a thieving steward is not desirable; he does wonder whether Ischomachos also teaches this sort of justice, i.e., as distinguished from the kind of justice that he teaches by rewarding the diligent and obedient workers and punishing the bad ones. Ischomachos does teach it, but apparently not all potential stewards whom he teaches with ease the other requirements of stewardship readily learn to be honest. This is not surprising, for according to Ischomachos, a potential steward should be passionately in love with lucre.[3] He teaches the justice in question by making use partly of the laws of Drakon and partly of the laws of Solon. To this extent he agrees with Socrates' view that there is no essential difference between despotic rule and rule over free men. Since he chooses the laws he applies from different codes, he acts the part of a legislator: the man capable of ruling is also a lawgiving man. Ischomachos' legislation is moderate: he keeps to the mean between

[1] Cf. XV.5.
[2] *Mem.* I.2.54.
[3] XII.15.

174

Drakon's and Solon's laws. Being a kingly man, Ischomachos does not hesitate to borrow some of the kingly laws, the laws of the king of Persia. He is silent about the laws to which he himself is simply subject; it goes without saying that he acts as a legislator on his estate only regarding such matters as have not been determined by the laws of his city. This is not to deny that that silence prepares in a manner the equivalence of the kingly and republican arguments in favor of farming set forth by Socrates in his conversation with Kritoboulos (Chs. IV–V). The kingly laws are in Ischomachos' view superior to other laws because they do not merely punish the wrongdoers but benefit the just men by making them richer; hence they induce even the passionate lovers of lucre to abstain from acting unjustly. Ischomachos is aware of the fact that even the best laws will not correct all men; those who are incorrigible are of course unfit to be made stewards. At the opposite pole from them stand those who act justly, not only because of the advantage they derive from it, but also because they desire to be praised by their master; Ischomachos treats these men like free men and honors them as perfect gentlemen.

The perfect gentleman Ischomachos is able to educate at least some of his stewards so that they become perfect gentlemen. This should not be too surprising, for, as we have learned earlier, there is no essential difference between a human being capable of ruling field hands and the kingly man. Without being aware of it, Ischomachos teaches Socrates that in order to be a perfect gentleman, one need not be wealthy, and not even free. Yet a perfect gentleman in the Ischomachean sense differs profoundly from the perfect gentleman in the Socratic sense. A perfect gentleman in the Socratic sense is a man who knows through thinking what is pious, what is impious, what is noble, what is base, and so on, or who considers thoroughly the just and unjust things.[4] Accordingly, in speaking of what is required of stewards, Ischomachos is completely silent about what one may call the intellectual qualities—about qualities which he had not failed to mention when speaking of what is required of the housekeeper.[5] The perfect gentlemen in Ischomachos' sense, and hence also the perfect stewards, must possess "ambitious natures"; they do not need to possess "good natures." [6] One would go too far were one to assert that there is no difference whatever between the perfect gentleman in Ischomachos' sense and the perfect steward. It suffices to remember Ischomachos' account of his activity as the citizen of a commonwealth. One may say that the gentlemanship of the stewards is akin to the gentlemanship of which subjects of tyrants are capable.[7]

The mere fact that the discussion of stewardship follows immediately the confrontation of the two ways of life (the Ischomachean and the Socratic) could induce one to consider the possibility that the discussion of stewardship continues and deepens that confrontation. It is obvious that Socrates is in no way engaged in educating human beings to stewardship. One could think, however, that he has this in common with the stewards and a fortiori with Ischomachos: he is a man capable of ruling. After all, he could do what he liked with any interlocutor. Yet, as Xenophon says, he could do this "in the speeches": [8] he could refute or silence all men who argued against him but could not induce all of them to obey him. It suffices to remember his accusers and condemners. This

---

[4] *Mem.* I.1.16, IV.8.4; cf. *Apol. Socr.* 3 and *Oec.* XI.22.
[5] IX.11–13.
[6] Cf. XIII.9 with *Mem.* IV.1.2.
[7] XI.23–24. Cf. *On Tyranny*, pp. 88–90.
[8] *Mem.* I.2.14; cf. *Mem.* IV.6.15.

"tragic" limitation of Socrates' power of speaking is, as it were, foreshadowed by its "comic" limitation, by Socrates' inability to persuade Xanthippe. For a variety of reasons these limitations do not become the theme in the *Oeconomicus*. Suffice it to say that in that work the wife is presented as the ruler of the husband rather than the husband as the ruler of the wife.[9] At any rate, Socrates differs from Ischomachos and his stewards by the fact that he is not a man capable of ruling. But in contradistinction to other "idle talkers," he knows both what it means to be a man capable of ruling and that he is not such a man.[10]

[9] VII.32 ff.

[10] Cf. *Anabasis* II.6.16–20 with Aristotle, *Eth. Nic.* 1180a1–21 and 1181a12–15.

⛩⛩⛩⛩⛩ Transition to the art of
farming (Chapter XV)

Apart from Chapter VI the present chapter is the only one devoted to the transition from one part of the work to another. Chapter VI presents the transition from the conversation with Kritoboulos to the conversation with Ischomachos. Chapter XV presents the transition from what one may call with some ambiguity or apparent exaggeration the discussion of gentlemanship to the discussion of the art of farming; the division of the Ischomachos section into a part devoted to gentlemanship and a part devoted to farming is as incisive as the division of the work as a whole into the Kritoboulos section and the Ischomachos section.

Socrates begins by enumerating the five qualities the perfect steward must possess. He knew by himself that the steward must be benevolent to his master and diligent, and he learned from Ischomachos that he must possess knowledge of the work to be done, that he must be capable of ruling, and that he must be just. In his enumeration Socrates replaces "just" by being as pleased as his master at exhibiting a rich harvest on the master's farm. One might say that he replaces justice, understood as abstaining from another man's property, by the apparently much loftier justice which consists in entirely subordinating one's own prosperity to the prosperity of someone else. Yet it would not be reasonable to expect the master to be just in this lofty sense toward his slaves. Let us be satisfied with the fact that Socrates here avoids speaking of justice. He is certain that the five qualities mentioned by him exhaust the subject, but he finds that one of them has not yet been sufficiently treated. Ischomachos does not know what Socrates has in mind; Socrates reminds him that he himself has said that not even diligence will be of any use if the steward does not know what work is to be done; in other words, Socrates points out that the central item in his enumeration has not yet been dealt with. Ischomachos did not know what Socrates had in mind, since he did not think that Socrates could be interested in farming.

Ischomachos understands Socrates to mean that he should teach him his art itself, the art of farming. Diligence and the other qualities discussed in the three preceding chapters are not arts. Art is a kind of knowledge, and knowledge of the work to be done and willingness to work are two different things.[1] But Ischomachos produces in his stewards benevolence toward himself, diligence, rulership, and even justice. Could knowledge of how to produce these things not be an art? Is that knowledge not an important part of the knowledge of how to manage one's household—of a kind of knowledge which is certainly an art, at least according to Socrates? Is not all virtue wisdom and knowledge? [2] Even if we had to grant that this is Socrates' view, it would not follow that it is Ischomachos' view. Even if we must leave open whether the good management of the household, i.e., the nonfortuitous increase of one's wealth, is an art, we must admit that one's wealth can be increased by the exercise of a great variety of arts, one of them the art of farming; farming might be an art, while increasing one's wealth is not. Socrates had recognized this state of things in a manner by calling Ischomachos' money-making [3] what Ischomachos now calls his art of farm-

[1] Cf. Plato, *Rep.* 374d5–6; *Mem.* III.9.14.
[2] I.1–2; *Mem.* III.9.5, IV.6.7.
[3] XI.11.

ing. Socrates says now that it is perhaps the art of farming which makes wealthy those who possess it. No one could blame Ischomachos for thinking that Socrates wishes to learn from him how to get rich by farming. But Ischomachos' way of getting rich is at the same time the apparently most important cognitive ingredient of his whole life. Even Ischomachos may wonder whether Socrates is not concerned with farming as a kind of knowledge rather than with getting rich.

Ischomachos praises his art on account of its "philanthropy" (love of human beings)—a quality which shows itself especially in the fact that farming is very easy to learn.[4] Socrates' response to this praise is astonishing: he acts as if he had not heard it; he pretends not to have heard it. He repeats his summary of the discussion of stewardship as well as his complaint about his and Ischomachos' failure to treat the kind of knowledge which stewards must possess, but his repetition is not literal. In the first place, he says now that the steward must be just. Second, he now supplements his complaint about the omission with a longish statement to the effect that by hearing that the steward must know what work he has to do and how and when to do it, Socrates would not know in any way how one ought to farm if he decided right now to farm. Does Socrates consider taking up farming? At any rate he now asks Ischomachos in so many words to teach him the works of farming. Confronted with this new situation, Ischomachos is compelled to respond in a new manner. His response consists again in a praise of the art of farming. He speaks again of how easy it is to learn that art: it is so easy to learn that Socrates could understand part of it by watching men doing farm work and the rest by hearing, so that he could teach another if he wished; as Ischomachos believes, Socrates already knows a

[4] Cf. XVIII.10 and XIX.17.

great deal about farming without being aware of the fact. One
wonders whether Ischomachos can see Socrates more easily as
a teacher of farming than as an actually farming man. Be this
as it may, he now adds a point of no mean importance: one
reason why farming, as distinguished from the other arts, is so
easily learned is that the farmers, as distinguished from the
practitioners of the other arts, do not conceal any feature of
their art; hence farming is superior to all other arts not only
on intellectual grounds (because it is so easy to learn) but on
moral grounds as well. One is tempted to say that the art of
farming surpasses all other arts because it makes the lowest demands on the intellect and the highest demands on character.
Surely a man circumstanced like Socrates can now no longer
avoid desiring to learn the art of farming. One must wonder,
however, whether farming can have its full moral effect if it is
not practiced. We are inclined to say that in his second praise
of his art Ischomachos emphasizes its justice, while in his first
praise he had stressed its philanthropy. At any rate, Socrates is
now fully satisfied with the praise of farming, with the fitting
proem to the speech on farming.

The nature of the land and the proper beginning of the account of farming (Chapter XVI)

This much is clear: Socrates will not be a farmer, i.e., a practicing farmer, a farmer "in deed." He may very well become an outstanding teacher of farming, a man who teaches farming through and through, most precisely, "in speech." As such he is exposed to a grave and even fundamental mistake, which Ischomachos does not hesitate to denounce right at the beginning of his account of farming. Those who treat farming, as we would say, only theoretically assert that in order to farm correctly, one must in the first place know the nature of the earth, i.e., of that part of the earth which one wishes to cultivate, the nature of one's land; as a consequence they regard at least the fundamental part of the art of farming as very complex, and hence, we may add, as equally susceptible of being concealed as the other arts: [1] the art of farming would not deserve the high praise bestowed on it by Ischomachos in the preceding chapter. It almost goes without saying that Socrates agrees with the theoreticians before he is enlightened by Ischomachos. He defends their view by saying that he who does not know what the land can bear is not likely to know what he should sow or plant; he who does not know the "nature" of the land, the "power" of the land, cannot in particular know its "power" to bear or to bring forth. Ischomachos rejoins that one can come to know what the land can and cannot bear by looking at the crops and the trees on a neighbor's land. He

[1] Cf. XVI.1 with *Mem.* III.5.14 and II.3.10.

182

seems to think that according to the theoreticians, impressed as they are by the great variety of soils, each farmer must first ascertain, before he begins to farm, the nature of his land, and he cannot do this by relying on what other men tell him about it, by relying on hearsay. But, he implies, land belonging to another man does not for this reason have another nature than one's own land. He thus achieves an emancipation from "one's own" which might remind us of the emancipation from "one's own" achieved later on by Socrates, near the beginning of his conversation with Kritoboulos.[2] Furthermore, by looking at the crops and trees on another man's land, one sees indeed what that land can produce; one does not thus see what it cannot produce; if Ischomachos were right, no innovation, no improvement in this particular province, would be possible. On the other hand, Ischomachos is right in saying that once one knows what one's land can and cannot bear, it is no longer useful to fight against the god or to expect the earth to bring forth and to nourish what she does not enjoy bringing forth and nourishing. Accordingly, he even comes close to correcting his previous error by saying that owing to the laziness of the owners, a given piece of land may not reveal its powers and that farmers may deliberately conceal the nature of their land. He disposes of this complication by concluding that even land that lies waste reveals its nature: if it brings forth wild products that are fine, it can, if tended, bring forth cultivated products that are fine; hence it remains true that men wholly inexperienced in farming can recognize the nature of any given land. (Did Ischomachos mean that precisely land that lies waste, that has not been modified in any way by art, reveals its nature?) Ischomachos thus succeeds in overcoming Socrates' original diffidence: Socrates will surely not abstain

2 I.3.

from farming out of fear that he does not know the nature of the land. His conviction is completed by his remembering right now that even fishermen—though their work is at sea and not at all on land—who look at the crops while sailing along at high speed, and while of course not stopping their boat for the purpose of observing, pronounce in most cases as correctly on the quality of the land (at least on its goodness) as the most experienced farmers.

It is fairly easy to see what is not the proper beginning of the account of farming: the proper beginning is not a disquisition on the nature of the land, except accidentally, in order to remove an error peculiar to mere theoreticians. But all men know prior to any instruction not only the nature of the land but many other things pertaining to farming,[3] and Ischomachos does not know which of these things Socrates knows already. More precisely, he is not likely to teach Socrates anything new to him; his teaching will rather consist of reminding Socrates of what he knows already. He asks him, therefore, from what point he should begin reminding him of farming. It is wrong to believe that Ischomachos refers to Socrates' view according to which teaching or understanding is remembering, for how should Ischomachos know of this view of Socrates? Above all, according to Ischomachos, the view that teaching is reminding or learning is remembering is correct only in the case of the art of farming.[4] Since, as we have seen, according to the *Oeconomicus*, Ischomachos is the teacher of Socrates in matters of the greatest importance, it is reasonable to say that, according to the same work, Socrates' later view of teaching and learning is the outcome of his meditation on a thought first suggested to him by the practice of the perfect gentleman par excellence.

[3] Cf. XV.10, end.
[4] XVIII.16-17.

Socrates replies to Ischomachos that, as it seems to him, he will gladly learn in the first place how he must cultivate the land in order to get, if he wishes, the greatest amount of barley and wheat: his desire to know this particularly becomes a man who is a philosopher (a lover of wisdom). This remark of Socrates calls for some attention, for it is the only remark on "philosophy" that occurs in the *Oeconomicus*. (In the *Hiero*, the parallel work, in which the wise man conversing with a ruler is a poet, "philosophy" is not mentioned at all; "poets" or "poetry" are mentioned in both works.) A philosopher, we gather, is not a man who unqualifiedly wishes to get the richest harvest of crops; nor is he a man who wishes to know how to get the richest harvest of crops merely for the sake of knowing this (or of teaching it); but he is a man who wishes to know it because he might wish to get such a harvest. The philosopher, it would seem, is a man characterized by a conditional or qualified love of lucre. This love might induce him under conditions not specified by Socrates to strive to get the greatest possible harvest of crops; more generally, it might induce him to become a farmer, or he might wish to become a farmer: under no circumstances does he wish to become a perfect gentleman, in the ordinary meaning of that expression. He is very eager to hear about Ischomachos' education of his wife, and yet he does not show the slightest desire to imitate Ischomachos in this respect; he is very eager to hear about Ischomachos' way of life in order to understand what it means to be a perfect gentleman; he does not show any serious desire to become a perfect gentleman himself.[5] He is more concerned with lucre than with perfect gentlemanship.[6] Ischomachos begins his account of profitable farming by beginning with the action that, as

[5] Cf. XVI.9 with VI.14, VII.9, X.1, XI.6–7, XV.9, and XV.13.

[6] Cf. the Platonic Socrates' vindication of the love of lucre in the *Hipparchus*.

Socrates knows, must precede sowing, namely, the preparation of the fallow land for sowing. Socrates also knows that no season other than spring is good for beginning to plow; Ischomachos draws the inference that spring is the only season good for beginning to plow. Similarly, master and pupil reach full agreement on the other points pertaining to the fallow.

▣▣▣▣▣ Sowing as well as reaping, threshing, and winnowing (Chapters XVII–XVIII)

It is not quite clear whether their agreement regarding the fallow is based in all points on the fact that both possess the required knowledge; perhaps on some points they only happen to have the same opinion.[1] At any rate they agree with one another. Ischomachos turns now to a subject regarding which not only he and Socrates but all men agree: the proper time for sowing. He asks Socrates whether, according to him, one ought to sow in the season which all men of the past and all men of the present, on the basis of experience, regard as the best for that purpose; for when the autumnal time comes, all men look toward the god in order to find out whether he will send rain and thus allow them to sow. Socrates replies that, according to all men, one ought not to sow while the earth is dry if one can help it, for those who did sow before the god commanded them to suffered many punishments. Whereas Ischomachos had only referred to men's dependence on the rain-sending god, Socrates interprets the bad consequences of men's disregard of the god as divine punishment; but he retracts that interpretation at the very moment he suggests it: men are sometimes compelled to sow even if the god has not given them his sign or his permission; Ischomachos' statement about the universal practice of mankind must be qualified accordingly. Ischomachos seems to be satisfied that there is universal agreement as to the properly qualified statement about

[1] Cf. XVII.1 with XVI.10–11, XVI.13, end, and XVI.14.

187

when to sow. Socrates gives the following reason for this universal agreement: what the god teaches brings about universal agreement; for instance, all men think that it is better in winter to wear warm clothing if they can and to light fire if they have wood. While the god teaches all men certain things good for them, he does not for this reason supply them with what they need in order to make his teaching useful to them: he may withhold from them these necessities. Ischomachos turns next to a subject regarding which there is no universal agreement, namely, the part of the rainy season that is most suitable for sowing. Socrates, who thus shows himself to be more of a theologian than the perfect gentleman, again gives the reason: the god does not manage the year in an orderly manner; hence in different years different parts of the rainy season are best for sowing. Must then all universal agreement, as well as the lack of it, be traced to the god or the gods? [2] Be this as it may, the Socratic statements just discussed are the only ones occurring in the Ischomachos section that set forth the Socratic theology.

Ischomachos now addresses a question to Socrates without telling him how all men answer it, and thus without almost compelling him to give the correct answer. Socrates' reply proves to agree with the reply that Ischomachos himself would have given. Neither the pupil nor the teacher refers here to the god or, in particular, to what the god teaches. It would be more than rash to infer that Socrates and Ischomachos genuinely agree only if they are not taught by the god or if their wisdom is only wisdom concerning human things, or human wisdom.

At this point Socrates addresses a question to Ischomachos for the first time in the section on farming and thus tacitly

[2] Cf. V.7 and V.12.

confesses his ignorance regarding one point of some importance. He asks him whether casting the seed requires a complicated art. He would not have asked this question if he had not
known in advance that seeds are cast. When Ischomachos re-
sumes again the leadership in the conversation and addresses a
series of questions to Socrates, it appears that Socrates knew
more about casting the seed than this philosopher might be
thought to know, for instance, that the seeds are cast (or
thrown) by the hand; yet it is not clear whether he knew before Ischomachos told him that some men can cast the seed
evenly and others cannot. From this fact Socrates infers that
sowers need practice no less than lyre players so that the hand
will obey the mind. Ischomachos cannot but agree. Does he
not thus admit that sowing—and a fortiori the whole art of
farming—is a complicated art and therefore not as philanthropic as he asserted it to be? In other words, even granted
that Socrates "knows," through hearing it from Ischomachos,
that the seed must be cast evenly, does he thus "know" how to
cast it evenly? Is not the "knowledge" of the art of farming
that he acquires through his conversation with Ischomachos
shot through with ignorance?

Ischomachos asks him next whether he would give the same
amount of seed to different soils regardless of whether the soil
is lighter or heavier, or to which kind of soil he would give
more. After Socrates has made sure that Ischomachos means
by lighter the same as weaker and by heavier the same as
stronger, he refers to his maxim according to which one must
give more to, or impose more on, the stronger; but he is perplexed, since he knows of cases in which one gives more to the
weaker in order to make it strong. Ischomachos must laugh
about the jocular manner in which Socrates states the alternative. He does not deny that there are ways of strengthening

weak land, but he leaves no doubt that one must give less seed to the weaker land or that Socrates would have hit on the correct answer by simply applying his maxim to the case at hand. But the point is that Socrates was uncertain whether the case at hand could be properly subsumed under his maxim. Not only is he unable to answer the question; he does not even raise the question.

Finally, Socrates again raises a question: For what purpose do you put hoers to work on the wheat? He must have seen hoers at work or at least have heard of them. Ischomachos leads him to understand the reason why one needs hoers by appealing partly to facts Socrates knows and partly to plausibilities. Socrates comes into possession of the correct answer through "hearing"—through being led to the correct answer by Ischomachos' leading questions—rather than through having seen.[3] He knows the whole art of farming partly from having seen men at work in the fields by which he passed and partly from having heard explanations given to him by Ischomachos. But, as we have seen, this knowledge is not genuine knowledge of the art of farming. He points to the character of his knowledge by an observation which he makes after Ischomachos had concluded his explanation of why one uses hoers. In his explanation Ischomachos had spoken of weeds and compared them to drones. This gives Socrates occasion to reflect on the importance of bringing in good likenesses, for by comparing the weeds to drones, Ischomachos had aroused Socrates' anger against the weeds much more than when he spoke of the weeds themselves. Socrates shows an interest in the art of rhetoric [4] of which Ischomachos gives no sign. His teaching of

[3] Cf. XV.10.

[4] *Mem.* I.2.15, I.2.31, I.2.34, IV.3.1, and IV.6.1. Xenophon is called "orator" in a considerable number of the manuscripts of his works, to say nothing of references to his art in treatises on rhetoric.

the art of farming, his exhorting Kritoboulos to exercise that art, is an act of rhetoric. Socrates exercised that art not only prior to his meeting with Ischomachos but also after it; yet after this fateful meeting his rhetoric serves the purpose, for instance, of making a gentleman farmer out of a gentleman farmer's son. To exhort men to the exercise of the art of farming one does not need solid knowledge of the art of farming; [5] the knowledge one acquires by looking at field hands doing their work and by having a single conversation with a gentleman farmer is more than adequate for this purpose, at least in the case of a man possessing a good nature. If we were blind to the seriousness behind Socrates' not altogether serious act, we would compare him to an excellent advertiser of cars who does not know how to drive a car, let alone how to manufacture one, and yet is inspired to write an impressive and not always ineffectual exhortation to buy cars by a single visit to a car factory, nay, to a showroom. Surely Socrates becomes an excellent exhorter to the art of farming, nay, to the whole art of household management thanks to a single conversation with a gentleman farmer, which takes place, not on the farm, but in a cloister of a temple in town. Or, if our comparison, however qualified, seems to be too much beneath the dignity of Socrates, let us at least confess that the people of Athens were not altogether inexcusable when they called a man who did not cease exhorting them to manage well the affairs of their households (or of the city), without ever practicing what he preached, an idle chatterer. Socrates' teaching of the art of household management is not quite serious. [6] This is not to

---

[5] Cf. Plato, *Gorgias* 454e3–456c7.

[6] The playful character of the *Oeconomicus* as a whole shows itself in the fact that terms designating laughter and joking occur, if my memory does not deceive me, twenty-two times in the *Memorabilia* and eighteen times in the *Oeconomicus*. In the *Memorabilia* only one

deny that the art of farming in particular may well be used as
a likeness of the art of rhetoric. But this does not mean that
the art of rhetoric itself is altogether serious. To see this, one
only has to compare it with the most serious of all arts or sciences, with theology.

The subjects following sowing—reaping, threshing, and winnowing—are all brought up by Socrates. He knows of their se-
quence prior to meeting Ischomachos. He knows that the corn
must be cut; he learns in what manner it must be cut and why
it must be cut in that manner by answering Ischomachos' questions; he answers them correctly, not because he had observed
reapers, but because the correct answers are practically inevitable. The discussion of threshing and winnowing has the same
character as that of reaping. Ischomachos easily visualizes Socrates as a cutter of wheat and as a winnower; so does Socrates
himself. Accordingly, Ischomachos draws the conclusion that
Socrates could even teach another man the quickest way to
winnow. Socrates is surprised at how much he knows, without
having been aware of it, of the works of farming and wonders
whether he does not similarly understand, without being aware
of it, and without ever having been taught them, such arts as
flute-playing. Yet Ischomachos denies that the conclusion from
the art of farming to any other art is valid: the art of farming
is the one most easy to learn. Socrates surprisingly concludes
this part of his instruction by saying that he was unaware of
his understanding of things pertaining to sowing; he thus reminds us of the defective character of his knowledge of that
part of the art of farming which was exhibited in the chapter
devoted to sowing.

case occurs in which Socrates is said to have made people laugh
(IV.2.5.); in the *Oeconomicus*, Socrates himself notes three cases of
this kind (II.9, VII.3, XVII.10).

𝕡𝕡𝕡𝕡𝕡 Planting (Chapter XIX)

Socrates retains the initiative. He asks Ischomachos whether the planting of trees, too, belongs to the art of farming. On Ischomachos' replying in the affirmative, Socrates wonders whether he could know the things pertaining to sowing and not know the things pertaining to planting, for it seems to have been established that he knows the art of farming, i.e., the whole art of farming; yet he is certain that he knows nothing of planting trees. His case seems to be the opposite of that of the younger Cyrus, who knew how to plant trees but perhaps not how to sow.[1] But Socrates' very enumeration of the things he does not know regarding planting shows that his ignorance in this respect is less than complete. Furthermore, as Ischomachos finds out by questioning him, Socrates has frequently seen how men plant trees; he shows him that what he has seen supplies the knowledge of the things pertaining to planting which he claimed not to know; even without being guided by Ischomachos, he finds out the reasons the planters act wisely in planting in the manner in which they plant; in finding out these reasons, he is helped by his previous knowledge of how rain and the sun affect the earth. Socrates thus proves to agree fully with Ischomachos regarding the planting of vines, although the vine is never mentioned here.[2] It appears that Socrates had no previous knowledge of the planting of fig trees, while he did know—without knowing that he knew—how olive

[1] Cf. IV.21–23.
[2] Socrates mentions the vine and its fruit altogether less frequently than Ischomachos (cf. especially XIX.18–19); cf. *Clouds* 417.

trees are planted, for they are commonly planted by the road-
side. He finally admits that he knows everything about planting, although to begin with, he did not believe that he knew
anything about it. Since he came to know of his knowledge
through answering Ischomachos' questions, he wonders
whether questioning—or rather the kind of questioning done
by Ischomachos—is not teaching; Ischomachos led him through
the things which Socrates knew, pointed out similarities between them and the matters which he did not believe he knew,
and thus persuaded him that he knew the latter as well as the
former. The reflection on whether teaching is questioning belongs as much to Socrates as distinguished from Ischomachos
as does the reflection on the power of likenesses in Chapter
XVII, but the practice to which the reflection refers and on
which it is based is Ischomachean: Socrates learns from Ischomachos' practice that teaching is questioning and is thus
brought on the way toward his discovery of dialectics in the
twofold meaning of the term.[3] Ischomachos, however, refuses
to accept Socrates' generalization: one could not teach Socrates the art of flute-playing, for instance, by questioning him, or
rather one could not persuade him that he knows how to play
flutes although he had never been taught to do it; one can
teach by questioning only the art of farming, the most philanthropic and gentle of all arts, i.e., the art that one can learn
most easily.

In reading the chapter on planting, one is struck by the fre-
quency with which the word "seeing" occurs; it occurs more
than twice as often in that chapter as in the rest of the section
devoted to farming. Equally peculiar to our chapter is the fre-
quency of Socratic oaths: Socrates, led by Ischomachos, is so

[3] *Mem.* IV.6.13–15. See pp. 147–148, above.

certain regarding the right kind of tree-planting because he has seen it so often. While Chapter XIX contains more Socratic oaths than any other chapter and not a single Ischomachean oath, the chapter containing the largest number of oaths—eight Ischomachean and three Socratic—is Chapter XII, the chapter opening the account of stewards. Just as Chapter XII is silent on piety, Chapter XIX is silent on theology. We are thus induced to wonder whether Chapter XII is not the beginning, and Chapter XIX the end, of one and the same section, the section on stewards. After all, the art of farming is practiced, and taught, by the stewards rather than the master himself; it is not Ischomachos who will teach the field hands how to cast the seed evenly. The section on stewards would then consist of two parts: a part devoted to the virtues of the stewards or to their gentlemanship and a part devoted to the art of farming. This bipartition would draw our attention to the fact that while all virtue is knowledge [4] and the art of farming is knowledge,[5] virtue and the art of farming are knowledge in very different senses. This is illustrated by the fact that the Socrates who converses with Ischomachos is less ignorant of the art of farming than of perfect gentlemanship in either the masterly or the stewardly forms (to say nothing more of his unrelieved ignorance of the art of managing one's wife). This makes it all the more necessary to wonder why Socrates did not apply his mind at all to what he had seen of farm work while passing by. The *Oeconomicus* suggests to us an answer: Socrates became concerned with the art of farming only after he had become interested in gentlemanship, farming being the art nearest and dearest to the perfect gentleman. One must also

[4] *Mem.* III.9.5, IV.6.7.
[5] I.1.

wonder why the *Oeconomicus* is so severely limited to agri-
culture and does not at all teach cattle-raising.[6] *Phyta*
("plants") has the same root as *physis:* by being concerned
with farming, Socrates continues, in a properly qualified and
subdued way, his early interest in *physiologia*. One may also
say that his early interest in *physiologia* survives in both the
theoteleology of the *Memorabilia* on the one hand and in the
teaching regarding farming of the *Oeconomicus* on the other.

[6] This failure is particularly striking in the light of *Mem.* IV.3.10. Cf.
especially *Oec.* V.3. Cf. pp. 117 and 123, above.

▦▦▦▦▦ The art of farming and love of farming (Chapter XX)

Socrates had turned to the art of farming because he thought that it is perhaps this art, this branch of knowledge, which makes its possessors wealthy and those who lack it poor.[1] In the meantime he has learned from Ischomachos that all men know equally well the things pertaining to farming. Hence all men (or all farmers) could be expected to do equally well. But in fact some farmers are very wealthy and others are very poor. This fact has more than one reason, one reason being divine dispensation.[2] Ischomachos does not have recourse to that reason.

While the section on farming (Chs. XV–XIX) was a dialogue between Ischomachos and Socrates in which Socrates learned how to farm by answering Ischomachos' questions, the two last chapters of the *Oeconomicus* consist again chiefly of "long speeches" of Ischomachos: Socrates has nothing, or almost nothing, of his own to contribute.

Ischomachos states that it is not the farmers' knowledge or ignorance that accounts for the fact that some of them are well off and others in dire need. Everyone knows for instance that the seed must be cast evenly and how to cast it evenly; yet it is not through casting the seed unevenly that households are ruined. Success or failure is due to diligence and care, or their lack, in doing the very simple things everyone knows

[1] XV.3.
[2] V.18–20.

ought to be done;[3] clever inventions are hardly of any account in this sphere. Ischomachos illustrates the crucial importance that diligence or care has in the most philanthropic of all arts by some examples taken from the highest of the warlike arts, from an art in which clever inventions can be eminently helpful, as Xenophon at any rate knew very well. Even in the art of strategy there are some simple rules which every general, not to say every man, knows, and yet these rules are frequently broken, owing to a lack of carefulness. To return to farming, some of the most important farm work is not only very easy to know but even very easy to do, and yet frequently neglected; the work in question is very easy to do since it is done chiefly by itself, thanks to the god above, to the mere passing of time, and to the pleasure which the earth takes in it. More than that: the theoreticians assert that the man who wishes to till the land must first know the nature of the land.[4] Ischomachos now grants that one may not be able to see what the land produces or to hear from anyone the truth about the land, but he contends that it is much easier for everyone to test the land than to test a horse and of course a human being; for the land does not in any way cheat but reveals its nature or power simply, without any disguise. Farming makes the lowest demands on men's knowledge, because its matter—the land, the earth—is the most honest, the most just of all beings. Precisely because the knowledge required for farming is easily available to everyone and therefore what makes the difference between the good and the bad farmer is not knowledge but diligence,[5] farming, or rather the earth which

[3] Observe the central position of viticulture in both XX.3 and XX.4. See the preceding chapter, n. 2.

[4] XVI.1–3.

[5] Lack of diligence or care is then characteristic of the second of the two kinds of farmers referred to in III.5–6 to whom Socrates promises

in its justice treats well those who treat it well, is the reliable accuser, not only of a bad farmer, but of a bad soul. Farming, Ischomachos seems to suggest, is the strongest power making for virtue. By suggesting this he does not mean to deny, as he makes quite clear, that the understanding of the other lucrative arts is compatible with honesty, but it is not clear what he thinks about the art of war as a source of wealth.[6] Finally, the diligence needed for making farming profitable is not only that of the master but that of his workers as well. This implies that the master must be diligent in making his workers diligent.

Here the question arises as to what it is that makes human beings diligent. When the stewards were discussed, it seemed that it is love of lucre that makes men diligent.[7] As regards the master, at any rate, Ischomachos offers a different explanation. His father had taught him both by his example and in so many words that to men who are capable of diligence and farm with utmost vigor, farming is the most effective way of making money. His father bought only run-down farms, for well-farmed land, he said, is very expensive to buy and, since it does not permit of improvement or progress, does not give one the great pleasure which goes with progress.[8] Ischomachos assures Socrates that by buying run-down farms and improving them thoroughly, he and his father increased the value of what they had bought many times. His father's invention is then very lucrative and at the same time so easy to understand that by just listening to its exposition on the part of Ischomachos, Socrates

to lead Kritoboulos; Kritoboulos is on his best way to becoming one of them (cf. III.7).

[6] Cf. I.15 with *Hipparchikos* 8.7–8.

[7] XII.15.

[8] Cf. *On Tyranny*, p. 105.

will understand it as well as he himself and could even teach it to another if he wished; Ischomachos does not expect Socrates himself to gain money through acting on this lesson; he is not even certain whether Socrates wishes to teach the lesson to others. According to Ischomachos' father, he owed his invention, and therefore all the diligence it demands, to his love of farming and his love of toil—to kinds of love that induced him to desire land permitting great improvement, in order to have something to do and to feel pleasure while being benefited. According to Ischomachos, his father was by nature the Athenian most in love with farming. After having learned from Ischomachos that his father sold the farms improved by him when he could get a good price and bought at once another run-down farm for very little money, and so on indefinitely, Socrates politely and jocularly rejects the son's view of the motive impelling his father. As he declares on his oath, i.e., in the greatest seriousness, men believe by nature that they love those things by which they believe they are benefited—just as most men believe that their benefactors are by this very fact good men.[9] Ischomachos' father believed himself benefited by his combination of farming and commerce; Socrates would have to know much more about him than he knows in order to say whether he was truly benefited by it; owing to an almost inevitable self-deception, he and his son believe that he loved that by which he believed himself benefited. What father and son believe to be love of farming was in fact love of gain.

Socrates had turned to Ischomachos in order to learn what perfect gentlemanship is or what the actions peculiar to the perfect gentleman are. Those actions include, just as do the actions of all other human beings, "economic" actions. The per-

[9] *Hellenica* VII.3.12.

fect gentleman is a farmer, if a gentleman-farmer. His motive is not so much gain as what is noble, what is becoming, what is conducive to the common good. Ischomachos, however, points to his father, who is a farmer and yet more than a farmer, a superfarmer, who uses farms as merchandise, for his motive proves to be love of gain. His motive could be satisfied by any lucrative enterprise. Ischomachos thus comes close to transforming economics, the management of one's landed estate, into chrematistics, the art or ability to increase one's money indefinitely.[10] He achieves the closest approximation to pure chrematistics that is possible on the basis of the previous choice of farming or the previous limitation to it. Since the gentleman is guided by the desire for honor rather than by the desire for gain,[11] Ischomachos comes close to abandoning perfect gentlemanship. He surely comes close to adopting the way of life opposite to the Spartan. Sparta is the only city that practices gentlemanship as a matter of public concern. Accordingly, while in the other cities all men devote themselves to money-making as much as they can by engaging in farming or in other lucrative pursuits, in Sparta free men are forbidden to have anything to do with money-making. On the other hand, Sparta thinks very highly of hunting.[12] As a consequence of Ischomachos' turn toward pure chrematistics, hunting occupies no important place in Ischomachos' way of life. Only one explicit mention of hunting occurs in the *Oeconomicus:* the land encourages hunting, since it affords the dogs a ready food supply and at the same time supplies food to the wild animals; the dogs, benefited by farming, benefit the countryside in their

[10] Consider that the Phoenician merchantman is to some extent a model for the order in Ischomachos' house.

[11] Cf. XIV.9.

[12] *Resp. Lac.* 4.7, 7.1–4, 7.6, 10.4. Cf. Plato, *Republic* 549a7 and context, and *Laws* 633b1–2.

turn by keeping the wild animals from injuring the crops and sheep and by helping to give safety to solitude.[13] This remark almost leaves one in doubt whether the hunting is done by the dogs alone or whether the master is supposed to join in. Be this as it may, the remark is made by Socrates; Ischomachos himself does not mention hunting at all except in an occasional derogatory remark about laggards who are "hunting soft breezes." [14] One could try to explain the silence of the *Oeconomicus* on hunting by the fact that love of hunting was held by some people to lead to the neglect of one's domestic affairs, of the management of one's household. In rejecting this opinion, Xenophon saves the cause of hunting only by pointing out that hunting is very useful for military training and that military strength is indispensable for the defense of the whole city and therefore also of one's own household: [15] he does not dare to assert that hunting is very lucrative.

Although Socrates jests about the love of farming allegedly animating Ischomachos' father, he does not disapprove of his lucrative practice and thus seems to approve of it and to recommend its imitation to Kritoboulos. He thus seems to go beyond the sacred line of perfect gentlemanship. One may go beyond this and say that he goes further than Ischomachos or his father in transforming economics proper into chrematistics. At the beginning of his conversation with Kritoboulos, which took place a considerable time after his conversation with Ischomachos, he defines the art of managing the household as the art of increasing one's wealth, without saying anything about any limitations to be imposed on that increase and in

[13] V.5–6. Cf. what Socrates says in *Mem.* II.9.2 on the dogs of Kritoboulos' father.
[14] XX.18.
[15] *Kynegetikos* 12.10–11.

particular about limitations imposed by justice. This is no doubt connected with the fact that in his comprehensive definition of household management which precedes the choice of farming, the individual's enriching himself by war, if not by tyranny, was not yet excluded.[16]

The change effected by Ischomachos is akin to a change effected by Xenophon's Cyrus. The old Persian polity in which Cyrus was raised in his early childhood was even more noble than the Spartan regime. The Persian nobles were supposed to spend practically their whole lives in town or in campaigns, i.e., not on their estates. In the first speech the adult Cyrus addressed to the Persian nobility, he persuaded them that virtue ought not to be practiced as it was hitherto practiced in Persia, for its own sake, but for the sake of great wealth, great happiness, and great honors.[17] That is to say, he persuaded them to cease being perfect gentlemen.[18]

With a view to a passage in the *Education of Cyrus* in which Xenophon praises the virtues of division of labor so as to "approach the division of labor within the workshop," Karl Marx speaks of Xenophon's "characteristic bourgeois instinct." [19] Marx does not pay sufficient attention to the fact that Xenophon's "instincts" were controlled by his admiration for Socrates. Or are Socrates and what he stood for only a part of the superstructure of a nascent or even merely divined bourgeois society? In order to find the true explanation of Xenophon's making his greatest concession to chrematistics in the *Oeconomicus*, one would have to consider the parallel work, the *Hiero*: in both works Xenophon experiments with

[16] I.15.

[17] *Cyrop.* I.5.7–10. Cf. *Cyrop.* I.2.4, I.2.8, I.2.9–11.

[18] Cf. Aristotle, *Eudemian Ethics* 1248b16–49a17.

[19] *Capital* (New York: Modern Library, n.d.), p. 402. Marx refers to *Cyrop.* VIII.2.4–6. But. cf. also *Cyrop.* VIII.2.20.

extreme possibilities—that of beneficent tyranny which was originally established by force and fraud on the one hand, and that of an economics which is about to become pure chrematistics on the other. By the former experiment he paves the way for Machiavelli; by the latter experiment he paves the way for certain post-Machiavellian thinkers. It goes without saying that Xenophon did not wish to experiment with both extreme possibilities in one and the same work. If any proof for this were needed, it would be supplied by the last chapter of the *Oeconomicus*.

The *Oeconomicus* teaches both perfect gentlemanship and the management of the household, especially the art of farming. As regards farming, we were assured that knowledge fulfills in it a rather minor function: not so much knowledge as diligence, assiduous practice, makes a man a good and successful farmer. Since the art of farming seems to be the most important cognitive ingredient of Ischomachos' way of life, one begins to wonder whether in gentlemanship, too, knowledge fulfills only a rather minor function, to say nothing of gentlemanship being knowledge. This difficulty is disposed of to some extent in the last chapter.

▨▨▨▨▨ The art of farming and the kingly man (Chapter XXI)

As Socrates now declares, he is perfectly satisfied with Ischomachos' well-done proof of his contention that the art of farming is of all arts the easiest to learn. Socrates is silent on the implications of that proof—implications which are none too flattering to perfect gentlemanship itself. Ischomachos is not clearly aware of this state of things, but, as the sequel shows, he now in fact vindicates the high rank, and in particular the high intellectual rank, of perfect gentlemanship. He does this altogether spontaneously, and Socrates remains altogether silent about that vindication. In the *Oeconomicus* the pupil is as silent about the concluding speech of the teacher as in the *Hiero*.

The high intellectual rank of farming is restored or established, according to Ischomachos, by the fact that farming, as well as politics, economics, and the art of war,[1] is in need of rulership, and as regards rulership Ischomachos claims to agree with Socrates in holding that the intellectual differences among men are of the utmost importance. Socrates had indeed spoken very highly of rulership in the central chapter of the section devoted to the stewards, yet he had not mentioned its intellectual ingredient; perhaps Ischomachos senses that Socrates would not spontaneously praise any human ability or activity in which the mind cannot be of great importance. Ischoma-

---

[1] Since farming is subordinate to economics, one may wonder whether politics is not subordinate to the art of war. Cf. the *Cyropaedia* as a whole.

chos first illustrates the virtue of rulership by the example of
the boatswain on a man-of-war; the good boatswain can say and
do such things as goad on the souls of the rowers toward toiling willingly; he and his subordinates are pleased with one another, whereas the bad boatswain and his subordinates come to
hate one another precisely because both the ruler and the ruled
are easygoing. Ischomachos next illustrates the virtue of rulership by the example of the general, to which he naturally
devotes much more space than to the first example. The generals who do not know how to rule at best make their soldiers
obey them through compulsion: they do not instill in them a
sense of honor. On the other hand, the rulers who are divine,
good, and in possession of the science of ruling can transform
the very armies demoralized by bad commanders into armies
ashamed to do anything disgraceful, proud to obey, and prepared to toil when toiling is called for. The good ruler, however, owes his being a good ruler not to his being the best soldier in the army—to the excellent condition of his body or his
marksmanship or horsemanship—but to his ability to inspire the
soldiers with eagerness to follow him through fire and through
every danger. The good rulers are justly called great-minded:
they do the great things they do by the mind rather than by
strength. After having ascended to the good general, Ischomachos descends for a short while to a humbler kind of ruler, the
stewards and the like, be they slaves or free men, who are in
charge of the farm work and to whom, if they are good at ruling, the prosperity of the household is due. He finally rises to
the highest height by describing the effect which the sudden
appearance of the good master has on the field hands—an appearance which is by no means unrelated to his power to harm
the bad field hands to the greatest degree and to honor the
zealous ones to the greatest degree: at the sight of him they

are stirred, and every one of them is filled with spirit and ri-
valry and love of excelling. Of such a man Ischomachos says
that he possesses some share of the character of the king. He
thus tacitly corrects Socrates' suggestion according to which
there is no essential difference between the master of slaves and
the king.[2] The ability by which the good master is distinguished is of the utmost importance for every kind of work
wherein something is achieved through human beings, and
therefore especially for farming. Of this ability Ischomachos
no longer asserts what he had so strongly asserted of farming,
that one can learn it partly by looking at farm work and
partly by hearing about it; instead he asserts that in order to
acquire this ability, one needs education ("culture"), a good
nature, and, above all, to have become divine. When speaking
of the education of the stewards to rulership, Ischomachos had
spoken, not of a "good nature," but of an "ambitious nature";
by his present remark he stresses again the profound difference
between the steward and the master, to say nothing of the
king. He explains his somewhat obscure statement about the
qualifications of the perfect master by saying that the master's
excellence does not at all seem to him to be altogether human
but that ruling over willing subjects is clearly something divine
that is given to those who have been truly initiated into the
mysteries of moderation: presumably only those who possess
education and a good nature can become, or have become,
truly initiated into the mysteries of moderation. But not all men
so initiated receive the crowning divine reward of actually becoming rulers over willing subjects. The relation between having been truly initiated into the mysteries of moderation and
having become divine reminds us of the relation, articulated by

[2] Cf. pp. 171 and 175, above.

Aristotle, between virtue as praiseworthy and happiness as worthy of honor or reverence or as a blessing.[3] Exercising tyrannical rule over unwilling subjects is no less a divine gift than ruling over willing subjects. But the former is given by the gods, as it seems to Ischomachos, to those whom they regard as worthy to live the life of Tantalus in Hades, of whom it is said that he spends unending time in fear that he will die a second time: the myth, or Ischomachos, assumes that people who have died fear dying much more than do those who have not yet died. The tyrant Hiero asserts that the tyrant spends night and day as if he were condemned by all human beings to die for his injustice.[4] Ischomachos does not speak of the injustice of the tyrant or of the justice of the good ruler, the ruler over willing subjects. He likewise does not make, as the Socrates of the *Memorabilia* does, rule under law or rule without law characteristics of the king or of the tyrant respectively.[5] But one may well say that the moderation of which he speaks so emphatically when praising the good ruler consists of justice and piety combined.[6]

Just as Chapter XX recommends the closest approximation to pure chrematistics that is compatible with perfect gentlemanship, Chapter XXI presents the closest approximation to kingship that is compatible with citizenship in a republic.[7] For every republic consists of households, and the households are ruled monarchically.

We conclude with a summary comparison of the *Oeconomi-*

---

[3] *Eth. Nic.* 1101b10–1102a4.

[4] *Hiero* 7.10.

[5] *Mem.* IV.6.12.

[6] *Mem.* IV.3.1–2, IV.4.1, IV.5.1.

[7] A study of the use and nonuse of *demos* and derivatives in the *Oeconomicus* and the *Hiero* might throw some new light on these two works.

cus and the *Hiero*, the only Xenophontic dialogues devoted to the teaching of arts, the economic art or the art of farming on the one hand, the tyrannical art on the other. Both dialogues are narrated by Xenophon. The *Oeconomicus* ends with strongly worded blame of the tyrant who rules over unwilling subjects. The *Hiero* ends with strongly worded praise of the tyrant who rules over willing subjects. But the happy tyrant praised at the end of the *Hiero* is a man who has in the past committed innumerable crimes, and his criminal past is not supposed to derogate from his future happiness. Clearly such a teaching could not be entrusted to Socrates: it is entrusted to the poet Simonides, a man who, in contradistinction to Socrates, is concerned with good living and with wealth, and who can always find refuge with a tyrant, since he is not attached to his fatherland. In both the *Oeconomicus* and the *Hiero* the wise man is presented partly as a teacher and partly as a pupil of a nonwise man. In the *Hiero* the wise man instructs a tyrant in the ways of beneficent tyranny after the tyrant had instructed him about the shortcomings of the tyrant's life. In the *Oeconomicus* the wise man instructs the son of a gentleman-farmer in both perfect gentlemanship and farming after a gentleman-farmer had instructed him in both subjects.

▣▣▣▣▣ Index of Authors

Andocides, 157 n.
Aristophanes, 83, 88, 91, 112, 127,
    159, 163-164, 166, 193 n.
Aristotle, 83, 122 n., 132 n., 161,
    162 n., 177 n., 203 n., 208

Bruns, Ivo, 133 n.
Burnet, John, 88 n.

Churchill, Winston, 100
Cicero, 96 n.

Dakyns, Henry G., 133 n.
Democritus, 136 n.

Gronovius, Jakob, 163 n.

Homer, 147 n.

Machiavelli, N., 84, 204
Marx, Karl, 203

Plato, 83, 88, 90 n., 102 n., 113 n.,
    119 n., 143 n., 148, 157 n., 161, 164,
    166 n., 167 n., 171 n., 179 n., 185 n.,
    191 n., 201 n.
Prodikos, 150, 155

Simonides, 131 n.

Thucydides, 83-84, 89

Winckelmann, J. J., 83 84